RAM - GOD OR GOOD GOVERNANCE

MANMEET SAINI

Made with ♥ on the Notion Press Platform
www.notionpress.com

Contents

Preface

The debate between religion and governance has been an ongoing discussion for centuries, with scholars and thinkers trying to determine the best approach to govern society. The role of religion and spirituality in governance has been a contentious issue, with some arguing that religion has no place in politics, while others claim that it is essential to establishing an equitable society. This book aims to explore the intersection between religion and governance through the lens of one of the most revered figures in Indian mythology - Lord Ram.

The book comprises several chapters, each addressing a specific aspect related to God, Creator & Lord Ram and his relevance to governance. Understanding the difference between God and Creator and the different philosophies attached to it, starting from the origins of Lord Ram, his birth, and the events that shaped his life, including his exile, his encounter with the demon king Ravana, and his eventual return to Ayodhya to exploring the ongoing debate between religion and governance, discussing the role of religion in politics and the challenges it poses to governance.

Focusing on Lord Ram's legacy as a symbol of good governance to various principles of governance embodied in the story of Lord Ram and their relevance to the present day including transparency, accountability, equity, and the rule of law.

The role of religion in governance, exploring the various ways in which religion can contribute to establishing an equitable society and further delve deeper into the debate between religion and governance, discussing whether Lord Ram is primarily a religious figure or a symbol of good governance.

Exploring the concept of Ram Rajya, which is often understood as a metaphor for an ideal society based on the principles of justice, equality, and good governance.

This book is an attempt to explore the intersection between religion and governance. It aims to contribute to the ongoing debate around religion and governance and to offer insights and perspectives that can inform our understanding of these important concepts. Whether Lord Ram is primarily a religious figure or a symbol of good governance, his story continues to inspire us and offers valuable lessons for establishing an equitable society.

Introduction

"Ram – God or Good Governance" is a book that explores the life of Lord Ram, one of the most revered deities in Hindu mythology, and his teachings on good governance. The book delves into the rich tapestry in multiple chapters understanding the philosophy and legacy.

As we all know once upon a time, in the ancient land of India, there lived a great king named Dasharatha. He had three wives, but he was childless, which made him deeply unhappy. One day, he performed a yagna, a sacred ritual, to please the gods and ask for a child.

The gods were pleased with Dasharatha's devotion, and they blessed him with four sons, born to his three wives. The eldest was named Ram, the second was Bharat, the third was Lakshman, and the fourth was Shatrughan. Ram was born to Dasharatha's first wife, Queen Kausalya, and was known for his virtues, wisdom, and strength.

As Ram grew up, he became famous for his archery skills and his kindness to all living beings. He was loved by the people of his kingdom, Ayodhya, and was adored by his brothers, who were devoted to him.

Dasharatha's second wife, Kaikeyi, demanded that her son Bharat be made the heir to the throne instead of Ram. She reminded Dasharatha of a promise he had made to her many years ago, and he had to fulfil it. Devastated by this turn of events, Ram, accompanied by his wife Sita and his brother Lakshman, went into exile for fourteen years.

During their journey, they met many sages and encountered many challenges, including a fierce battle with the demon king Ravana. With the help of his loyal monkey army and his divine weapons, Ram defeated Ravana and rescued Sita from his captivity.

After the exile ended, Ram returned to Ayodhya, where he was welcomed by his people with great joy. He was crowned as the king, and he ruled his kingdom with wisdom, compassion, and justice. He taught his people the importance of dharma, karma, and the virtues of leading a virtuous life.

Ram's life and teachings have been immortalized in the epic poem, the Ramayana, which is still revered and recited in India today. His legacy and significance continue to inspire millions of people around the world, and his story has influenced art, literature, and culture in many countries.

However, controversies and debates surrounding Lord Ram have also arisen, such as the debate around his birthplace and the criticism of his treatment of Sita. Despite this, his story remains a powerful and enduring symbol of courage, righteousness, and devotion to duty.

Ram, is often viewed as a manifestation of the divine. His story highlights the power of faith and the importance of upholding moral values, even in the face of adversity. The concept of God, similarly, has been a source of contemplation and inquiry across cultures and religions. While the nature and existence of God remain open to debate, the influence of religious beliefs and spiritual experiences, such as those encountered by Ram during his journey, cannot be denied. Whether viewed through the lens of mythology or philosophy, Ram and the idea of God continue to spark reflection and contemplation about the role of the divine in our lives.

People have been seeking answers to the question, "Does God exist?" for as long as they can remember. Some believe in the existence of an all-powerful, all-knowing deity who created the universe and everything in it. Others reject the idea of God altogether, citing a lack of evidence or conflicting beliefs. Regardless of where you stand on the topic, the question of God's existence has remained a fundamental and complex one.

The concept of God has existed in various forms and across cultures and religions. The Abrahamic religions of Judaism, Christianity, and Islam all believe in a single, all-knowing, all-powerful God who created the universe and governs it. Eastern religions like Hinduism, Buddhism, and Taoism have a more nuanced view of God, with multiple deities and a focus on personal enlightenment and inner peace.

The philosophy of God has been a topic of debate among philosophers for centuries. Some argue that the existence of the universe itself is proof of a divine creator, while others believe that the complexity of life can be explained by scientific theories like evolution. The question of whether believing in God is necessary for moral behaviour is also a philosophical one.

The nature of God is another aspect of the debate. Different religions and cultures have different views on God's attributes and characteristics. Some believe in an all-loving and benevolent deity, while others view God as a more judgmental and punishing figure. The relationship between science and religion is also an area of discussion, with some arguing that the two can coexist, while others view them as incompatible.

One of the most significant challenges to the idea of God is the problem of evil. If God is all-powerful and all-loving, why do evil and suffering exist in the world? This is a question that has perplexed philosophers and theologians for centuries.

Despite the debates and controversies, many people report personal experiences with God, from feeling a sense of divine presence to having spiritual awakenings. These testimonies and spiritual journeys add another layer to the discussion about God's existence and significance.

In conclusion, the question of God's existence has fascinated and divided people for centuries. The concept of God takes many forms across cultures and religions, and the debate over God's nature, existence, and role in the world will likely continue for generations to come.

The existence of God and the idea of a creator are closely related concepts that have fascinated humans for centuries. While the existence of God is a more broad and complex question that encompasses various beliefs and philosophies, the idea of a creator typically focuses on the origin and nature of the universe. Both concepts have been explored by religious, scientific, and philosophical perspectives, the concept of God and the idea of a creator have played a significant role in shaping human culture and understanding of the world.

Many different cultures and belief systems around the world shared a common belief in the existence of a creator. Some believed in a single omnipotent deity who created the universe and all living things, while others believed in multiple gods who each had a role in the creation and governance of the world.

As time passed, scientific theories emerged to explain the origins of the universe. The Big Bang Theory became the most widely accepted theory, but it also left many unanswered questions about the nature of the universe and its origin.

Religious and philosophical views on the creator continued to be explored, with Christianity, Islam, Judaism, Hinduism, Buddhism, and other belief systems each offering their unique perspective. While they shared some similarities, such as the belief in a higher power who created the universe, there were also differences in how they conceptualized the creator's nature and purpose.

One of the most significant challenges to the idea of a benevolent creator was the problem of evil. If a creator exists who is all-knowing and all-powerful, how can they allow the existence of evil and suffering in the world? Various attempts were made to reconcile this problem, such as the idea that suffering is necessary for spiritual growth, or that it is a result of human free will.

The role of free will was explored in various views of the creator, with different interpretations of what it means and its relationship to the concept of a creator. Some saw free will as a gift from the creator, while others saw it as a burden that could lead to evil and suffering in the world.

Contemporary debates on the concept of the creator continue to this day, with scientific, philosophical, and theological debates on the topic. New ideas and developments are constantly emerging, pushing the boundaries of our understanding of the universe and its origins.

The concept of the creator has significant implications for many aspects of human life and society, from ethics to politics to spirituality. It continues to be a source of inspiration, wonder, and debate, shaping the way we see ourselves and our place in the world.

In the context of the idea of the creator, the concept of good governance raises questions about the role of the divine in the governance of the world, and how ethical and moral principles should be upheld. The concept of the creator can be seen as a guiding force in the pursuit of good governance, as it provides a moral framework for ethical decision-making and social responsibility.

Chapter four of the book is all about the principles of good governance. It starts by providing an overview of what good governance is, why it matters, and what principles and values underpin it. Good governance is the effective and efficient management of resources and affairs of a nation or organization, and it is critical for social, economic, and political stability. The principles that underpin good governance include transparency, accountability, rule of law, participation and civic engagement, responsiveness, anti-corruption and ethics, public sector reform, local governance and decentralization, and international dimensions of good governance.

The chapter goes on to explain the importance of transparency and accountability in good governance and provides examples of how these principles can be put into practice in various contexts. Transparency refers to the openness and accessibility of information, while accountability means taking responsibility for actions and decisions. The chapter emphasizes the need for the rule of law as a cornerstone of good governance and explores different dimensions of this concept such as legal certainty, access to justice, and the role of courts and other legal institutions.

The chapter also highlights the importance of citizen participation and civic engagement in good governance and discusses different ways in which people can be involved in decision-making processes at various levels. It emphasizes that governments and other institutions must be responsive to the needs and preferences of the people they serve and discusses different strategies for ensuring responsiveness.

Anti-corruption measures and ethical standards are also essential in good governance. The chapter discusses the role of these principles in promoting good governance and provides examples of how they can be applied in different contexts.

The chapter also discusses public sector reform, the challenges and opportunities associated with it, and different strategies for improving the effectiveness and efficiency of government institutions. It emphasizes the importance of local governance and decentralization in good governance and examines different models and approaches for devolving power and resources to the local level.

Finally, the chapter explores the international dimensions of good governance, including the role of international organizations, treaties, conventions, and other forms of global governance. It summarizes the key themes and ideas covered in the chapter and looks ahead to future challenges and opportunities for promoting good governance around the world. It provides a comprehensive and detailed analysis of the principles of good governance, emphasizing the importance of transparency, accountability, rule of law, citizen participation, responsiveness, anti-corruption measures and ethical standards, public sector reform, local governance and decentralization, and international dimensions of good governance. It highlights the critical role that good governance plays in promoting social, economic, and political stability and outlines strategies for achieving it.

The principles and values embodied by Lord Ram have transcended religious boundaries and have become universal symbols of good governance. Lord Ram is known for his adherence to dharma, the righteous path, and his commitment to justice, fairness, and compassion for all. These principles align with the core principles of good governance, such as transparency, accountability, participation, and responsiveness to the needs of citizens. By applying these principles in their governance, leaders can promote sustainable and inclusive development, reduce corruption, and build trust between government and citizens. Thus, Lord Ram's legacy is not limited to a religious figure but rather serves as an inspiration for all leaders to strive towards ethical and effective governance.

The multifaceted role of Ram in Hinduism and beyond begins by highlighting his significance in Hinduism and the key themes and ideas that delve into different aspects of Ram's story and its interpretation across various domains. In the section on Ram in literature, the many different literary works featuring Ram as a central character are explored, including the Ramayana, the Mahabharata, and various other texts from across the Indian subcontinent.

The section on Ram in philosophy examines the philosophical underpinnings of Ram's story and explores how different schools of Hindu philosophy interpret and understand his role in the world. The historical context in which Ram's story emerged is explored in the section on Ram in history, examining how it was influenced by the social, political, and cultural forces of its time.

How Ram has been depicted in art, sculpture, and other forms of visual culture are explored in the section on Ram in art and iconography, and the different representations are examined to understand what they tell us about his place in Hindu society and culture.

The section on Ram in popular culture looks at the various ways in which Ram has been adapted and reinterpreted in popular culture, including in films, television shows, and other forms of media. In the section on Ram as a symbol of national identity, the chapter explores how Ram has been invoked as a symbol of national identity and unity in modern India, and the political and cultural debates surrounding his use in this context.

How different religious and political groups have used Ram's story to advance their agendas are explored in the section on Ram and the politics of belief, and the tensions and conflicts that have arisen as a result are examined. The section on Ram and contemporary religious practice examines how Ram continues to be worshipped and venerated by millions of Hindus around the world and explores what his story means to people in different contexts and communities The key themes and ideas covered throughout reflect on what Ram's story can teach us about religion, culture, and the human experience more broadly.

The qualities of governance that make Ram a symbol of perfection are often associated with his portrayal in religious texts, but they also have relevance beyond religious contexts. For example, Ram is known for his commitment to justice, truthfulness, and integrity, which are universally recognized as essential qualities of good governance. His emphasis on dharma, or righteous conduct, can be seen as a call for ethical and responsible leadership. Ram's ability to inspire loyalty and devotion among his followers is also a testament to his leadership qualities, including his communication skills and his ability to lead by example. In this way, Ram's story can serve as a model for effective and ethical governance, not only for those who follow his religion but for all those who seek to lead with integrity and compassion.

The qualities of governance that make Ram a symbol of perfection and his story are relevant to the topic of governance.

Exploring Ram's leadership qualities, including his integrity, fairness, courage, and compassion. These qualities are examined in the context of governance and how they make Ram a symbol of perfect governance. The author delves into Ram's approach to justice, which was grounded in the principles of fairness, equity, and impartiality. This approach is explored in detail, and the author explains how it can inform contemporary governance practices. Further examining how Ram managed resources, including finances, human resources, and natural resources. The author explains how Ram's approach to resource management can be applied in modern governance. Exploring Ram's relationship with citizens, including how he listened to their needs, engaged them in decision-making, and maintained transparency and accountability.

Ram's reign as king was characterized by good governance practices, including rule of law, accountability, and participation. His legacy continues to inform contemporary governance around the world. Ram's story has influenced Indian political thought and governance practices, including the role he plays in contemporary debates over secularism, diversity, and democracy.

Comparing Ram's approach to governance to other historical and contemporary leaders and governance models from around the world, highlighting the similarities and differences between them. Understanding Ram's legacy includes debates over his treatment of women and marginalized groups, and how these critiques can inform ongoing efforts to improve governance practices.

Reflecting on what Ram's story can teach us about governance, leadership, and the human experience more broadly.

The relevance of Ram Rajya in promoting a sustainable and inclusive world lies in its emphasis on good governance principles that prioritize the well-being of all individuals and the environment. This is evident in the qualities of governance that make Ram a symbol of perfection. Ram Rajya is characterized by principles of justice, fairness, accountability, and respect for human rights, all of which are essential for promoting sustainable and inclusive development.

In Ram Rajya, the ruler is expected to serve the people selflessly, listen to their needs, and act in the interest of the common good. This is reflected in the story of Ram's exile, where he voluntarily gave up his throne to uphold his father's promise, and his devotion to his subjects, exemplified by his famous dialogue "Janani Janmabhoomischa Swargadapi Gariyasi" (Mother and motherland are greater than heaven). By promoting a governance model that puts the well-being of the people and the environment first, Ram Rajya can serve as a model for sustainable and inclusive development that promotes the welfare of all individuals and ensures a better future for generations to come.

Further explaining its significance in Hinduism and highlighting the key themes and ideas to discuss how the principles of Ram Rajya, such as justice, fairness, compassion, and righteousness, are universal values that are relevant to all religions and faiths. It explores how Ram Rajya embodies ethical principles that are shared across different religions and faiths, and how these principles can inform contemporary ethical debates and challenges.

Ram Rajya, such as the rule of law, accountability, and participation, can inform good governance practices that are relevant to all religions and faiths. It highlights how Ram Rajya prioritized social justice and equity and how these principles can be applied to address contemporary social and economic inequalities.

Furthermore, explores how Ram Rajya was characterized by a deep respect for the environment and the natural world and how this perspective can inform contemporary environmental ethics and practices. It also discusses how the principles of Ram Rajya can foster interfaith dialogue, understanding, and cooperation and how they can contribute to building a more peaceful and harmonious world. Ram Rajya is rooted in the principle of nonviolence, and how this principle can inform contemporary efforts to promote peace and conflict resolution. It also examines criticisms and controversies surrounding the idea of Ram Rajya, including critiques of its historical and cultural context, how these critiques can inform ongoing efforts to apply its principles in contemporary contexts and how Ram Rajya can serve as a source of inspiration and guidance for people of all religions and faiths who are committed to building a more just, peaceful, and sustainable world.

The construction of Ram Mandir and the ideals of Ram Rajya share a common thread in their emphasis on promoting an inclusive and sustainable society based on the principles of good governance, making them both significant symbols of progress and unity for people across different communities and backgrounds.

The Ram Mandir in Ayodhya embodies the principles of ideal governance in various ways. Firstly, the symbolism of the Ram Mandir, including its architecture, design, and religious practices, reflects principles such as social justice, environmental sustainability, cultural heritage, and interfaith relations.

Moreover, the Ram Mandir can serve as a symbol of social justice and equity by promoting religious tolerance and unity. It also embodies the principles of environmental sustainability by using renewable resources and traditional building methods, contributing to economic development by attracting tourists and promoting local industries.

Additionally, the Ram Mandir's preservation can promote cultural identity and pride, while fostering interfaith dialogue, understanding, and cooperation, contributing to building a more peaceful and harmonious world.

Lastly, the Ram Mandir embodies the principles of good governance, including transparency, accountability, and citizen participation, making it an ideal model for good governance.

Despite criticisms and controversies surrounding the Ram Mandir, it remains a powerful symbol of India's cultural heritage and the principles of ideal governance. By upholding these principles, India can continue to build a more peaceful, prosperous, and equitable future for all its citizens.

CHAPTER ONE

About Ram

Lord Ram, also known as Rama, Ramachandra, Maryada Purushottam, Raghuveer and many more names is one of the most revered deities in Hinduism. He is considered to be the seventh avatar or incarnation of Lord Vishnu, who is one of the three main deities in Hinduism along with Lord Brahma and Lord Shiva.

Lord Ram's life is chronicled in the Hindu epic, the Ramayana. According to the Ramayana, Lord Ram was born in Ayodhya, a city in northern India, to King Dasharatha and Queen Kaushalya. He was born during the Treta Yuga, an ancient period in Hindu mythology.

As a young prince, Lord Ram was known for his wisdom, compassion, and bravery. He was married to Sita, a princess from the kingdom of Mithila, who was known for her beauty and virtue.

Lord Ram was exiled from his kingdom for 14 years due to a conspiracy by his stepmother, Kaikeyi. During his exile, Lord Ram faced numerous challenges and obstacles, including battles with demons such as Ravana and his army of rakshasas.

The most famous event in Lord Ram's life is his victory over Ravana, the king of Lanka, who had kidnapped Sita. With the help of his loyal devotee, Hanuman, and an army of monkeys, Lord Ram waged war against Ravana's forces and emerged victorious.

Lord Ram is revered as the embodiment of dharma and is considered to be an ideal son, husband, and king. His life and teachings continue to inspire millions of people around the world, and his story has been adapted into numerous works of art, literature, and film. He is worshipped by millions of Hindus worldwide and his birthday, known as Ram Navami, is celebrated with great fervour and devotion every year.

Birth and Childhood

King Dasharatha's quest for an heir was a significant theme in his life. He had three wives, but none of them had borne him any children. Worried about his legacy, he approached his guru, Vasishtha, for guidance. Vasishtha suggested that King Dasharatha perform a yagna, a sacred ritual, to please the gods and seek their blessings for a child.

Following Vasishtha's advice, King Dasharatha performed the yagna, and as a result, he was blessed with four sons. Lord Ram was the eldest of them and was born to King Dasharatha's first wife, Queen Kaushalya.

Lord Ram's birth was celebrated with great joy and enthusiasm in Ayodhya. His virtues were apparent from a very young age. As a child, he was kind-hearted, compassionate, and wise beyond his years. He was deeply devoted to Lord Vishnu and spent much of his time meditating and praying.

As a child, Lord Ram was known for his exceptional qualities. He was wise beyond his years, and his intelligence was unmatched. He was also known for his humility, courage, and compassion. He was adored by the people of Ayodhya and was favoured by his father.

One of the most well-known incidents of Lord Ram's childhood is the story of how he broke the bow of Lord Shiva. King Janaka, the ruler of the kingdom of Mithila, held a competition to choose a husband for his daughter, Sita. The competition involved breaking the bow of Lord Shiva, which had been given to King Janaka by the gods.

Many princes tried to break the bow, but none were successful until Lord Ram arrived. He picked up the bow and easily broke it, impressing everyone present. King Janaka was so impressed with Lord Ram that he agreed to marry his daughter, Sita, to him.

Another significant event in Lord Ram's childhood was his encounter with the demoness Tadaka. Tadaka was terrorizing the forest near Ayodhya and causing chaos. Lord Ram, along with his younger brother Lakshman, defeated Tadaka and restored peace in the forest.

Lord Ram's childhood was filled with various adventures and accomplishments, all of which were marked by his virtues and his adherence to dharma. He was deeply devoted to Lord Vishnu, and his piety and devotion earned him the respect and admiration of all who knew him.

Overall, Lord Ram's birth and childhood set the foundation for his life as a hero and a great ruler. His qualities and virtues, which were apparent even as a child, would help him overcome the challenges he would face in the future and establish him as one of the most revered deities in Hinduism.

Exile and Journey

Lord Ram's exile and journey to the forests is a significant part of the Ramayana, one of the two major epics of Hindu mythology. The following is a detailed account of this part of his life:

Lord Ram was living happily in Ayodhya with his wife, Sita, and his younger brother, Lakshman, when his father, King Dasharatha, was forced to banish him to the forest for 14 years. This was because of a promise he had made to one of his wives, Kaikeyi, years earlier.

Lord Ram, Sita, and Lakshman left Ayodhya and travelled southward to the Dandaka forest. Along the way, they met several sages and other characters who would play important roles in their journey.

The first sage they met was Bharadwaj. He advised them to stay in Chitrakoot, a scenic spot on the banks of the river Mandakini, where they could live peacefully in the forest.

While living in Chitrakoot, Lord Ram met several other sages, including Atri and Anasuya. They welcomed him warmly and gave him valuable advice. Lord Ram also met Jatayu, a vulture who became a loyal friend and ally.

However, Lord Ram's peaceful existence in Chitrakoot was interrupted when the demoness Surpanakha, Ravana's sister, arrived. She was attracted to Lord Ram and wanted to marry him. When he refused her advances, she attacked Sita. In response, Lakshman cut off Surpanakha's nose, which infuriated Ravana and led to his decision to kidnap Sita.

After this incident, Lord Ram, Sita, and Lakshman left Chitrakoot and continued their journey through the forests. They encountered several other sages and hermits, including Agastya, who gave Lord Ram powerful weapons to use against Ravana.

Lord Ram's journey through the forests also brought him into contact with Hanuman, the monkey god, who became a loyal devotee and ally. Hanuman would later play a crucial role in rescuing Sita from Ravana's captivity.

Eventually, Lord Ram and his companions arrived at Panchavati, a place near the river Godavari. They built a small hut there and lived a peaceful life for some time. However, their peaceful existence was once again disrupted when Ravana, the demon king of Lanka, abducted Sita.

Lord Ram's journey to the forests was marked by his piety, courage, and devotion to dharma. He encountered several challenges and obstacles along the way but faced them with grace and fortitude. His interactions with the various sages and characters he met helped him grow spiritually and prepared him for the challenges that lay ahead.

Sita and Marriage:

His marriage to Sita is considered one of the most significant events in his life.
The story begins with King Janaka of Mithila, who was performing a Yajna or a sacrifice ceremony to please the gods. During the ritual, he found a baby girl in a furrow of the field, whom he named Sita. As she grew up, she became known for her beauty, intelligence, and virtues.

Meanwhile, Lord Ram, along with his brothers, was sent on a fourteen-year exile to the forest by his stepmother Kaikeyi, who had been manipulated by her maid. During their exile, Lord Ram and his brothers encountered various challenges, including battles with demons and other supernatural creatures.

One day, Lord Ram and his brother Lakshman came across the hermitage of Sage Valmiki, where they met Sita. Lord Ram was struck by her beauty and fell in love with her at first sight. They soon got married in a grand ceremony in Mithila, which was attended by many notable personalities from across the country.

However, their happiness was short-lived as soon after the marriage, Lord Ram was called upon to go to war with Ravana, the demon king of Lanka, who had abducted Sita. With the help of an army of monkeys led by Hanuman,

Lord Ram was able to defeat Ravana and rescue Sita from his captivity.

Despite being reunited, Lord Ram and Sita faced several challenges in their lives. After returning to Ayodhya, Lord Ram was crowned king, and Sita became his queen. However, soon after their coronation, a rumour spread that Sita had been unfaithful to Lord Ram during her captivity. To prove her purity, Sita agreed to undergo a trial by fire, and by the grace of the gods, emerged unscathed.

Despite the successful trial, Lord Ram was plagued by doubts about Sita's purity, and eventually, he asked her to leave the palace and go into exile. Sita, who was pregnant at the time, went into the forest and gave birth to twin sons, Luv and Kush. They were raised by Sage Valmiki, and when they grew up, they reunited with their father and reconciled with him.

Throughout his life, Sita played a significant role in Lord Ram's life, serving as his loyal and devoted wife. Her devotion and sacrifice have made her a beloved figure in Hindu mythology, and her story continues to inspire millions of people to this day.

Victory over Ravana

The story of Lord Ram's battle against the demon king Ravana is one of the most well-known and revered stories in Hindu mythology. According to the epic poem, the Ramayana, Lord Ram, accompanied by his loyal army of monkeys and bears, waged war against Ravana to rescue his wife Sita, who had been abducted by the demon king.

Lord Ram's victory over Ravana was not only a triumph of good over evil but also a demonstration of strategic thinking and wise leadership. Here are some of the strategies Lord Ram used in the battle:

- Building alliances: Lord Ram realized that he could not defeat Ravana alone and needed the support of other powerful beings. He built alliances with the monkey king Sugriva, his commander Hanuman, and other animals like bears, eagles, and squirrels, who all joined his army.

- Knowing the terrain: Before entering Lanka, Lord Ram sent Hanuman to gather information about the terrain and the enemy's strengths and weaknesses. This allowed him to plan his strategy and take advantage of the terrain during the battle.

- Deception: Lord Ram used deception to trick Ravana and his army. For instance, he created a fake army of monkeys and bears by tying flaming torches to their tails and releasing them into the forest. Ravana's army mistook them for a real army and attacked them, giving Lord Ram's army an advantage.

- Targeting the enemy's weak points: Lord Ram identified Ravana's weak points and targeted them. For instance, he killed Ravana's brother Kumbhakarna, who was his strongest ally, first. He also killed Ravana's son Indrajit, who had the power to make himself invisible, by using an arrow that had been blessed by the goddess Brahma.

The battle between Lord Ram and Ravana teaches us several valuable lessons. One of the key lessons is the importance of good over evil. Lord Ram was a virtuous and righteous leader who fought to rescue his wife and protect his people. The story also emphasizes the importance of alliances and teamwork in achieving success. Lord Ram's army included beings of different sizes and strengths, but they worked together towards a common goal.

Additionally, Lord Ram's strategic thinking and wise leadership demonstrate the importance of planning, knowing the terrain, and identifying the enemy's weaknesses. These are crucial skills in any battle or conflict, whether on the battlefield or in our personal or professional lives. Finally, the story also teaches us the importance of faith, courage, and perseverance in the face of adversity. Lord Ram's unwavering faith in the divine and his determination to succeed, even in the face of seemingly insurmountable challenges, serve as an inspiration to us all.

Return to Ayodhya

After Lord Ram's victory over Ravana, he returned to Ayodhya with Sita and his army of monkeys and bears. His return was celebrated with great joy and fanfare by the people of Ayodhya, who had been eagerly awaiting his return.

Lord Ram's coronation as the king of Ayodhya was a grand event. He was crowned with the blessings of the sage Vashishta and other revered sages, and his rule was marked by peace, prosperity, and justice. During his reign, he taught several important lessons on governance and leadership, which continue to inspire people even today.

Here are some of the key teachings of Lord Ram on governance and leadership:

- Upholding Dharma: Lord Ram's rule was marked by his commitment to upholding Dharma, the righteous way of living. He believed that a ruler's duty was to serve the people and maintain order and justice in society. He ensured that his subjects lived happy and prosperous life and that justice was dispensed fairly.

- Leading by example: Lord Ram believed that a leader should lead by example. He lived a simple and humble life and was always accessible to his people. He was known for his fairness and kindness and treated everyone equally, regardless of their status.

- Listening to advice: Lord Ram believed in seeking advice from his advisors and considering different perspectives before making a decision. He valued the opinions of his ministers, sages, and other wise men and women and was known for his wisdom and prudence.

- Treating everyone with respect: Lord Ram believed in treating everyone with respect and compassion, regardless of their background or status. He was known for his empathy and understanding and was always willing to help those in need.

- Balancing compassion with firmness: Lord Ram believed that a ruler should be compassionate but firm when needed. He was known for his firmness in dealing with wrongdoers but also showed compassion towards those who had repented for their actions.

The story of Lord Ram's return to Ayodhya and his coronation as the king teaches us several valuable lessons on governance and leadership. It emphasizes the importance of upholding Dharma, leading by example, listening to advice, treating everyone with respect, and balancing compassion with firmness. These lessons are relevant even today, and leaders can learn a lot from Lord Ram's teachings on governance and leadership.

Philosophy and Teachings

Lord Ram is a revered figure in Hinduism and is regarded as an embodiment of virtue, wisdom, and righteousness. His life and teachings have been a source of inspiration for people for centuries. Here are some of Lord Ram's philosophical teachings:

- Dharma: Lord Ram believed in the importance of dharma or righteousness. He upheld dharma and followed it even in the most challenging situations. He considered dharma as the foundation of human existence, and he believed that by following dharma, one could achieve both material and spiritual success.

- Karma: Lord Ram believed in the law of karma, which states that every action has consequences. He emphasized the importance of performing one's duties without worrying about the outcome. He believed that one should focus on doing the right thing, and the results would take care of themselves.

- Virtuous Life: Lord Ram believed that leading a virtuous life is essential for achieving happiness and inner peace. He stressed the importance of leading a life that is guided by values such as honesty, compassion, and self-control. He believed that by cultivating these virtues, one could attain spiritual enlightenment.

- Service to others: Lord Ram believed in serving others, and he considered it one of the highest forms of spiritual practice. He believed that by serving others, one could transcend the ego and attain a state of selflessness.

- Faith and devotion: Lord Ram emphasized the importance of faith and devotion. He believed that by having faith in God and surrendering to Him, one could overcome the challenges of life and attain spiritual liberation.

In conclusion, Lord Ram's teachings emphasize the importance of leading a virtuous life, following dharma and performing one's duties without worrying about the outcome. His teachings continue to inspire people to this day and serve as a guide for leading a meaningful and fulfilling life.

Legacy and Significance

Lord Ram's legacy and significance in Hindu mythology and Indian culture are immense. He is regarded as one of the most important and revered figures in Hinduism, and his life and teachings have inspired people for centuries. Here are some of how Lord Ram's legacy and significance are reflected in Hindu mythology and Indian culture:

- The Ramayana: The Ramayana is one of the most significant religious texts in Hinduism, and it tells the story of Lord Ram's life and his triumph over evil. It is believed to have been written by the sage Valmiki, and it is a source of spiritual inspiration for millions of people.

- Festivals: There are many festivals and traditions associated with Lord Ram, the most significant of which is the festival of Diwali. Diwali is a five-day festival that celebrates Lord Ram's return to Ayodhya after defeating the demon king Ravana. It is also a celebration of light over darkness, good over evil, and knowledge over ignorance.

- Temples: There are many temples dedicated to Lord Ram across India, and they are popular pilgrimage sites for devotees. The most famous of these is the Ram Janmabhoomi temple in Ayodhya, which is believed to be the birthplace of Lord Ram.

- Significance in Indian culture: Lord Ram is an important figure in Indian culture, and his teachings and values have had a profound impact on Indian society. His emphasis on dharma, karma, and leading a virtuous life continues to be a source of inspiration for people.

- symbol of unity: Lord Ram is also seen as a symbol of unity and brotherhood in India. His story transcends religious and cultural boundaries and is celebrated by people of all faiths and backgrounds.

In conclusion, Lord Ram's legacy and significance in Hindu mythology and Indian culture are immense. His story continues to inspire people, and his teachings and values have had a profound impact on Indian society. His message of righteousness, selflessness, and devotion continues to be relevant even today, making him a timeless figure in Indian culture and history.

Ramayana in other cultures:

Yes, the Ramayana has had a significant influence on various cultures, particularly in Southeast Asia and South Asia. Here are some examples of how the Ramayana has influenced these cultures:

- Southeast Asia: The Ramayana has had a profound impact on Southeast Asian cultures, particularly in countries such as Thailand, Indonesia, and Cambodia. In these countries, the Ramayana is a popular theme in traditional dance, music, and theatre. The story of Lord Ram is also depicted in many temples and monuments across these countries.

- South Asia: The Ramayana has also influenced various cultures in South Asia, particularly in countries such as Nepal and Sri Lanka. In Nepal, the Ramayana is celebrated through the festival of Dashain, which marks the victory of Lord Ram over Ravana. In Sri Lanka, the story of the Ramayana is an important part of the country's culture and history, and there are many temples dedicated to Lord Ram across the country.

- Literature: The Ramayana has also inspired many works of literature in various languages, including Hindi, Bengali, Tamil, and Malayalam. These literary works have helped to spread the story of Lord Ram to a wider audience and have played an important role in preserving the Ramayana's cultural significance.
- Art and Architecture: The Ramayana has also had a significant impact on art and architecture in various cultures. Many temples, monuments, and artworks across South Asia and Southeast Asia depict scenes from the Ramayana, and these works of art have helped to preserve the story and cultural significance of Lord Ram.

In conclusion, the Ramayana has had a significant influence on various cultures, particularly in Southeast Asia and South Asia. Its cultural significance continues to be celebrated and preserved through various art forms, literature, festivals, and traditions.

CHAPTER TWO

Existence of God

The concept of God is one of the most complex and debated topics throughout history, with many different interpretations and definitions depending on cultural, religious, and philosophical perspectives. However, I will provide a general overview of some common characteristics and definitions of God:

- Creator: Many religious traditions view God as the creator of the universe and everything within it. God is often considered the ultimate source of all life and existence.
- Omnipotent: God is often seen as all-powerful, possessing unlimited power and control over the universe and all that it contains.

- Omniscient: God is often considered all-knowing, possessing infinite knowledge of everything that has happened, is happening, and will happen.

- Omnipresent: God is often seen as present everywhere at all times, transcending the limitations of time and space.

- Eternal: God is often considered timeless, existing outside of time and space and beyond the limitations of mortality.

- Loving: Many religious traditions view God as a loving and compassionate being, who cares deeply for all of creation and desires the best for all.

- Just: God is often considered a just and fair judge, who rewards good behaviour and punishes wrongdoing.

- Personal: Some religious traditions view God as a personal being who can be known and communicated with through prayer and spiritual practices.

- Transcendent: God is often considered to be beyond the limitations of human understanding and experience, existing beyond the physical world.

These are just a few of the many characteristics and definitions of God, and there are countless interpretations and perspectives on this topic depending on cultural, religious, and philosophical perspectives.

The Concept of God Across Cultures and Religions

The concept of God varies across cultures and religions, and there are countless interpretations and beliefs about the nature and attributes of God. Here are a few examples:

- Christianity: In Christianity, God is seen as a triune God consisting of the Father, Son, and Holy Spirit. God is seen as the creator of the universe and all life within it and is characterized by qualities such as love, mercy, and justice.

- Islam: In Islam, God is known as Allah and is seen as the one and only true God. Allah is characterized by qualities such as mercy, justice, and omnipotence, and is believed to have created the universe and all life within it.

- Judaism: In Judaism, God is seen as the creator of the universe and all life within it. God is characterized by qualities such as mercy, justice, and compassion, and is believed to have made a covenant with the Jewish people.

- Hinduism: In Hinduism, some many gods and goddesses represent different aspects of the divine. The ultimate reality, known as Brahman, is seen as the source of all existence and is characterized by qualities such as love and compassion.
- Buddhism: In Buddhism, the concept of God varies depending on the tradition. Some Buddhist traditions do not believe in a personal God, while others see the Buddha as a divine being. The ultimate goal in Buddhism is to achieve enlightenment and liberate oneself from suffering.

These are just a few examples of how the concept of God varies across cultures and religions. The beliefs and practices associated with God can be deeply personal and significant to individuals and communities.

The Abrahamic God:

The Abrahamic God is the God worshipped by Jews, Christians, and Muslims. Each of these religions has its own specific beliefs and practices associated with the Abrahamic God, but there are also many similarities in how God is understood and worshipped across these traditions.

In Judaism, the Abrahamic God is known as Yahweh or Jehovah. God is seen as the creator of the universe and all life within it and is characterized by qualities such as love, mercy, and justice. The Jewish scriptures, including the Torah, guide us for living by God's will. Central to Jewish belief is the idea of a covenant between God and the Jewish people. This covenant is seen as an agreement in which God promised to protect and bless the Jewish people, and in return, the Jewish people would obey God's commandments.

Some key beliefs about God in Judaism include:

- God is one: Judaism is a monotheistic religion, which means that it believes in only one God.
- God is personal: In Judaism, God is seen as a personal being who can be known and communicated with through prayer and spiritual practices.
- God is just: Jewish tradition teaches that God is a fair and just judge who rewards good behaviour and punishes wrongdoing.
- God is loving: Despite being just, God is also seen as loving and compassionate, caring deeply for all of creation and desiring the best for all.

In Christianity, the Abrahamic God is known as the Father, Son, and Holy Spirit. God is seen as the creator of the universe and all life within it and is characterized by qualities such as love, mercy, and justice. The teachings of Jesus and the Bible guide us for living by God's will. Central to Christian belief is the idea of salvation through faith in Jesus Christ. This means that Christians believe that by placing their faith in Jesus and following his teachings, they can be saved and receive eternal life in heaven.
Some key beliefs about God in Christianity include:

- God is one: Like Judaism, Christianity is a monotheistic religion that believes in only one God.

- God is triune: Christianity teaches that God is one, but also exists in three persons: the Father, Son, and Holy Spirit.

- God is personal: In Christianity, God is seen as a personal being who can be known and communicated with through prayer and spiritual practices.
- God is loving: Christians believe that God's love for humanity is so great that he sent his son, Jesus, to die on the cross to save humanity from sin.

In Islam, the Abrahamic God is known as Allah. Allah is seen as the one and only true God, who is characterized by qualities such as mercy, justice, and omnipotence. The teachings of the prophet Muhammad and the Quran guide living by God's will. Central to Islamic belief is the idea of submission to God's will, and the belief that all humans are equal in the eyes of God.

Some key beliefs about God in Islam include:

- God is one: Like Judaism and Christianity, Islam is a monotheistic religion that believes in only one God.
- God is transcendent: In Islam, God is seen as beyond human understanding and experience, existing beyond the physical world.
- God is merciful: Islamic tradition teaches that God is merciful and forgiving and that seeking God's forgiveness is an important part of worship.
- God is just: Like Judaism, Islam teaches that God is a fair and just judge who rewards good behaviour and punishes wrongdoing.

In summary, the Abrahamic God is a central figure in the religions of Judaism, Christianity, and Islam. While there are differences in how God is understood and worshipped across

Eastern Views of God:

Hinduism, Buddhism, and Taoism

Eastern religions have diverse views of God, with each religion having its unique concepts and understandings. Here are some of the key beliefs about God in Hinduism, Buddhism, and Taoism.

Hinduism is a polytheistic religion that has a vast pantheon of gods and goddesses. The ultimate reality in Hinduism is Brahman, which is considered to be the supreme, all-encompassing, and eternal essence that pervades everything in the universe. Brahman is beyond human comprehension and is seen as the source of all existence. In Hinduism, each of the gods and goddesses is a manifestation of Brahman and represents different aspects of the ultimate reality.

Some key beliefs about God in Hinduism include:

- God is one: Despite the vast number of gods and goddesses in Hinduism, there is a belief in one ultimate reality that underlies all existence.

- God is personal: Hindus believe in personal gods and goddesses that can be worshipped and communicated with through prayer and rituals.

- God is loving: Hinduism teaches that God is compassionate and loving and that devotion to God can lead to liberation from the cycle of birth and death.

- God is immanent: Brahman is believed to be present in all things, including every individual and every object in the universe.

Buddhism does not have a concept of a personal God but rather focuses on the individual's spiritual journey towards enlightenment. Instead of worshipping a deity, Buddhists seek to follow the teachings of the Buddha, who is seen as a spiritual teacher rather than a god. Buddhism recognizes that there are gods and goddesses in the universe, but they are not seen as the ultimate reality or the path to enlightenment.

Some key beliefs about God in Buddhism include:

- God is not the focus: Buddhism does not focus on the concept of God or gods, but rather on the individual's spiritual journey towards enlightenment.

- God is not necessary: Buddhism teaches that individuals can achieve liberation and enlightenment without the need for a deity or divine intervention.
- God is not permanent: In Buddhism, all things are seen as impermanent and constantly changing, including gods and goddesses.

- God is not the ultimate goal: The ultimate goal of Buddhism is to achieve enlightenment, which is a state of complete liberation from suffering and the cycle of birth and death.

Taoism is a philosophy and religion that originated in China, and is centered around the concept of the Tao, which means "the way". The Tao is seen as the ultimate reality and source of all existence. In Taoism, there is a belief in a pantheon of gods and goddesses, but they are seen as manifestations of the Tao rather than individual entities.

Some key beliefs about God in Taoism include:

- God is not separate: Taoism teaches that everything in the universe is interconnected and part of the same source, including gods and goddesses.

- God is not necessary: Taoism does not require belief in a deity or divine intervention for spiritual growth or enlightenment.

- God is not anthropomorphic: In Taoism, gods and goddesses are not seen as anthropomorphic or human-like, but rather as symbolic representations of natural phenomena and cosmic forces.

- God is not the ultimate goal: The ultimate goal of Taoism is to live in harmony with the Tao and achieve inner peace and balance.

In summary, Eastern religions have diverse views of God, with Hinduism having a polytheistic belief system centred around the concept of Brahman, Buddhism not focusing on the concept of God and instead emphasizing the individual's journey towards enlightenment, and Taoism emphasizing the interconnectedness of all things and the ultimate reality of the Tao.

The Philosophy of God:

The philosophy of God is a branch of metaphysics that deals with the nature and existence of God. Philosophers have offered various arguments for and against the existence of God, and here are some of the key arguments.

Arguments for the Existence of God:

- Cosmological Argument: This argument posits that everything in the universe has a cause and that there must be a first cause, an uncaused cause, which is God. This argument is based on the idea that the universe could not have come into existence on its own, and that there must be a cause outside the universe.

- Teleological Argument: This argument is also known as the argument from design, and it posits that the complexity and order of the universe suggest the existence of an intelligent designer, which is God. The teleological argument is based on the idea that the universe has a purpose and that there must be a designer who created it with a specific purpose in mind.

- Ontological Argument: This argument posits that the very concept of God implies his existence. It suggests that God's existence is necessary and that it is impossible to conceive of God not existing. This argument is based on the idea that God's existence is inherent in the concept of God itself.

Arguments against the Existence of God:

- Problem of Evil: This argument posits that the existence of evil in the world is incompatible with the existence of an all-powerful, all-knowing, and all-loving God. The argument suggests that if God is all-powerful, he could eliminate evil, if he is all-knowing, he would know how to eliminate evil, and if he is all-loving, he would want to eliminate evil. Therefore, the presence of evil in the world suggests that God does not exist.
- Argument from Ignorance: This argument posits that just because we cannot prove that God does not exist, it does not mean that he does. It suggests that the burden of proof is on those who claim that God exists and that until such proof is provided, we cannot assume the existence of God.
- Inconsistency Argument: This argument posits that the concept of God is inconsistent with itself. It suggests that the idea of an all-powerful, all-knowing, and all-loving God is self-contradictory, as the existence of evil in the world is incompatible with the idea of an all-loving God. Therefore, the concept of God is logically inconsistent and cannot exist.

The philosophy of God is a complex and contentious area of metaphysics. Arguments for the existence of God are based on ideas such as causation, order, and necessity, while arguments against the existence of God are based on ideas such as evil, ignorance, and inconsistency. These arguments continue to be debated by philosophers and theologians, and no single argument has been able to conclusively prove or disprove the existence of God.

God and Ethics:

Moral Implications of Believing in God

The relationship between God and ethics is a complex and multifaceted issue. On one hand, many religious traditions believe that God provides the ultimate source of morality and that ethical behaviour is derived from obedience to God's commandments. On the other hand, some philosophers argue that morality can be derived from reason and logic, and that belief in God is not necessary for ethical behavior.

Here are some of the key moral implications of believing in God:

- Divine Command Theory: This theory posits that moral truths are derived from the commands of God. According to this view, actions are morally right or wrong simply because God commands or prohibits them. In this sense, belief in God provides a basis for morality, as his commands are considered the ultimate source of ethical behaviour.

- Moral Objectivism: Belief in God often implies a belief in objective moral standards. According to this view, moral truths exist independently of human beliefs or desires and are grounded like God himself. This view holds that ethical behavior is not a matter of subjective opinion, but is based on universal, objective principles that apply to all people at all times.

- Accountability and Punishment: Many religious traditions believe that God holds people accountable for their actions and that there are consequences for immoral behaviour. This belief provides a powerful incentive for ethical behaviour, as individuals are motivated to act by God's commands to avoid punishment or gain reward.

- Moral Community: Belief in God often creates a sense of community and shared values among believers. This sense of community can provide support and encouragement for ethical behaviour, as individuals are held accountable by their peers for their actions.

However, there are also criticisms of the idea that belief in God is necessary for ethical behaviour:

- Euthyphro Dilemma: This philosophical problem, named after the Platonic dialogue, asks whether something is good because God commands it, or if God commands it because it is good. If the former, then morality becomes arbitrary and dependent on God's whims. If the latter, then morality exists independently of God and belief in God is not necessary for ethical behaviour.

- Human Reason: Many philosophers argue that morality can be derived from human reason and logic, and that belief in God is not necessary for ethical behaviour. They argue that moral principles can be discovered through rational inquiry, observation, and reflection on human experience.

- Moral Diversity: Religious beliefs and practices vary widely across different cultures and traditions. This raises questions about the universality of moral principles derived from belief in God, as different cultures may have different ideas about what constitutes ethical behaviour.

In conclusion, the relationship between God and ethics is complex and multifaceted. While belief in God can provide a basis for morality, it is not necessary for ethical behaviour. Additionally, the idea that morality is based on divine command raises philosophical problems, such as the Euthyphro Dilemma. Ultimately, the relationship between God and ethics is a topic of ongoing debate among philosophers, theologians, and believers.

The Nature of God:

Attributes and Characteristics

The nature of God is a topic of intense philosophical and theological debate, and different religious traditions and philosophical schools of thought have put forth various ideas about God's attributes and characteristics. Here are some of the key attributes and characteristics associated with God:

- Omnipotence: God is often described as all-powerful and able to do anything logically possible. This means that God is not limited by physical or natural laws, and can intervene in the world in miraculous ways.

- Omniscience: God is often described as all-knowing and having complete knowledge of everything that has happened, is happening, and will happen. This means that God has perfect knowledge of all events and all people, and can see the future as well as the past.

- Omnipresence: God is often described as being present everywhere at once. This means that God is not limited by physical space, and can be present in all places at all times.

- Eternality: God is often described as being eternal, meaning that he exists outside of time and has no beginning or end.

- Goodness: God is often described as being perfectly good and morally pure. This means that God is the source of all goodness and that his nature is inherently good.

- Justice: God is often described as being perfectly just and fair. This means that he judges all people based on their actions and intentions, and rewards or punishes them accordingly.

- Love: God is often described as being loving and compassionate. This means that he cares for all people, and desires their well-being and happiness.

- Transcendence: God is often described as being beyond human understanding and the physical universe. This means that he is not limited by the laws of nature, and exists outside of the material world.

Of course, these attributes and characteristics are not universally agreed upon, and different religious traditions and philosophical schools of thought may have different ideas about the nature of God. Additionally, the concept of God is so vast and complex that it is impossible to fully capture it in words or ideas. Nonetheless, these attributes and characteristics provide a starting point for understanding the nature of God.

God and Science:

How Science and Religion Interact

The relationship between science and religion, specifically regarding the existence of God, has been a topic of much debate for centuries. Here are some ways in which science and religion interact about God:

- The conflict thesis: The conflict thesis posits that science and religion are fundamentally incompatible and that they are in constant conflict. This view is often associated with figures like Galileo and Darwin, who were seen as challenging religious dogma with scientific discoveries. However, many scholars today reject the conflict thesis as an oversimplification of the complex relationship between science and religion.

- Complementarity: Complementarity refers to the idea that science and religion are different ways of understanding the world and that they complement each other rather than being in conflict. According to this view, science provides empirical evidence about the natural world, while religion provides a moral framework for understanding our place in it. Some theologians argue that God is the source of both science and religion and that they are both valid ways of understanding the world.

- Theistic evolution: Theistic evolution is the idea that God created the world and its natural processes, including evolution. This view holds that science and religion are not in conflict, but rather that they provide different perspectives on the same reality. Theistic evolution is a popular view among many Christians and is also embraced by some other religious traditions.

- Non-overlapping magisteria: Non-overlapping magisteria (NOMA) is the idea that science and religion are separate domains of knowledge that do not overlap. According to this view, science deals with empirical observations and testable hypotheses, while religion deals with questions of morality, meaning, and purpose. Proponents of NOMA argue that each domain of knowledge should be respected in its own right and that they should not be in conflict.

It's worth noting that while science and religion can interact in many ways, they operate on fundamentally different epistemological foundations. Science relies on empirical observation and testable hypotheses, while religion relies on faith and revelation. As a result, they often approach questions of existence, meaning, and purpose in very different ways. Nonetheless, many scholars argue that they can be complementary and that they do not need to be in conflict.

The Problem of Evil

The problem of evil is one of the most pressing and difficult theological and philosophical questions concerning the existence of God. The basic problem is this: if God is all-powerful, all-knowing, and perfectly good, then why does evil exist in the world? How can God allow suffering and injustice?

There have been numerous attempts to address this problem over the centuries, but no single answer has been universally accepted. Here are some of the key ideas and arguments that have been put forth:

- Free will: One popular response to the problem of evil is the free will defence. According to this view, God created humans with free will so that they could choose to do good or evil. While this freedom allows for the possibility of evil, it is necessary for genuine moral agency and for humans to freely choose to love God. However, critics of this argument argue that it does not fully account for natural disasters or suffering that seem to be caused by forces beyond human control.

- Theodicy: Theodicy is the attempt to justify God's ways in the face of evil. There are many different theodicies, but they generally fall into two categories: those that appeal to the greater good that can come from evil, and those that appeal to the limitations of human understanding. For example, some argue that suffering can bring about greater empathy and compassion, or that it is necessary for humans to grow and develop spiritually. Others argue that humans simply cannot comprehend God's ways and that the existence of evil is part of a larger plan that we cannot fully understand.

- Non-existence of God: Some argue that the existence of evil proves that God does not exist. If God were truly all-powerful and all-good, the argument goes, then he would not allow evil to exist. However, proponents of this argument often overlook the possibility that God has a larger plan or that there are limits to his power.

- Mystical approaches: Some religious traditions take a mystical approach to the problem of evil, arguing that suffering is ultimately an illusion and that God's ways are ultimately beyond human comprehension. For example, some Buddhist traditions argue that suffering is caused by our attachment to impermanent things, and that true liberation comes from letting go of these attachments.

The problem of evil remains one of the most difficult and debated questions in theology and philosophy. While there are many different approaches and arguments, none are entirely satisfying or conclusive. Ultimately, it may be a question that can never be fully answered, and that requires us to grapple with the limits of human understanding and the mysteries of the universe.

Personal Experiences with God

Personal experiences with God, often referred to as spiritual or religious experiences, can take many different forms and are highly subjective. These experiences can range from feelings of inner peace or connection to something greater to visions or revelations that fundamentally alter a person's understanding of the world and their place in it. Many people who have had such experiences describe them as profound, transformative, and life-changing.

Testimonies are one way in which people share their personal experiences with God. These are often deeply personal stories of how individuals have come to know and experience God in their lives. Testimonies can be found in many religious traditions, including Christianity, Judaism, Islam, and others. In some cases, testimonies may involve a conversion experience, where an individual describes a moment of spiritual awakening that led them to embrace a particular faith or way of life. In other cases, testimonies may describe a gradual process of coming to understand and connect with God over time.

Spiritual journeys are another way in which people describe their experiences with God. These journeys may involve a search for meaning and purpose in life, or a desire to deepen one's connection to the divine. They may also involve a process of questioning and exploring different religious traditions and beliefs, to find a path that resonates with one's own experiences and values. Some spiritual journeys may be more inwardly focused, while others may involve engaging with a particular religious community or seeking out the guidance of a spiritual teacher or mentor.

While personal experiences with God are highly subjective and can vary greatly from person to person, they can also be deeply meaningful and transformative. For many people, these experiences provide a sense of comfort, guidance, and purpose in life, and help to connect them with something larger than themselves. They may also inspire individuals to engage in acts of service, compassion, and social justice, as a way of living out their faith and responding to the needs of the world. Ultimately, personal experiences with God can be a source of strength, inspiration, and hope, as individuals seek to navigate the challenges and complexities of life.

Who is God and What Does It Mean for Us?

The question of who God is and what it means for us has been explored and debated for centuries across different cultures and religious traditions. While there are many different ideas and beliefs about God, one common thread is the recognition of a higher power or force that transcends the limitations of human existence and provides a sense of meaning and purpose in life.

For many people, belief in God provides a sense of comfort, guidance, and hope, particularly in times of difficulty or uncertainty. It can also inspire individuals to engage in acts of compassion, service, and social justice, as they seek to live out their faith and make a positive difference in the world.

At the same time, the concept of God has also been the source of significant debate and disagreement, particularly about issues of morality, justice, and the problem of evil. Some people have questioned the existence of God altogether, while others have sought to reconcile their faith with the challenges and complexities of the world around them.

Ultimately, the question of who God is and what it means for us is a deeply personal one, shaped by our individual experiences, beliefs, and values. While we may never fully understand the nature of God, or agree on the many different interpretations and understandings that have emerged throughout history, we can continue to explore and reflect on this question, as we seek to live meaningful and purposeful lives and make a positive impact in the world around us.

CHAPTER THREE

The Concept of the Creator

The Concept of the Creator

The concept of the Creator refers to the idea of a higher power, deity or divine being that is responsible for the creation and maintenance of the universe and all that exists within it. This concept is central to many religions and spiritual traditions, providing believers a sense of meaning, purpose, and direction.

The belief in a creator is often based on a combination of faith, personal experience, and philosophical or metaphysical reasoning. In many traditions, the creator is considered to be omniscient, omnipotent, and benevolent, possessing qualities that are beyond human understanding. The creator is often depicted as a loving, caring, and compassionate figure who guides and protects humanity.

In some religions, the creator is seen as a single entity, while in others, there may be multiple creators or a pantheon of gods and goddesses. The concept of the creator can also vary greatly in terms of the relationship between the creator and the created. Some religions see the creator as separate and distinct from the world, while others view the creator as an intrinsic part of all that exists.

The concept of the creator has played a significant role in shaping human culture, morality, and ethics. It has been the source of inspiration for many works of art, literature, and music. For believers, the concept of the creator offers a sense of comfort, hope, and purpose, as they believe that they are part of a larger cosmic plan and that their lives have meaning and significance.

However, the concept of the creator has also been a source of controversy and conflict throughout history. Different religions and spiritual traditions have different ideas about the nature and attributes of the creator, leading to disputes and disagreements. Some people reject the concept of the creator altogether, seeing it as a relic of an outdated and superstitious worldview.

The concept of the creator is a complex and multifaceted idea that has played a significant role in shaping human culture and spirituality. While it is a source of comfort and inspiration for many believers, it is also the subject of debate and controversy among people of different beliefs and worldviews.

Defining the concept of a creator and its significance in various cultures and belief systems

The concept of a creator is the idea of a higher power or divine being responsible for the creation and maintenance of the universe and all that exists within it. This idea is central to many cultures and belief systems worldwide and has been a source of inspiration, hope, and comfort for countless people throughout history.

In many religions, the creator is seen as an omniscient, omnipotent, and benevolent deity who is responsible for the creation and sustenance of the world. In some traditions, the creator is a single entity, while in others, there may be multiple creators or a pantheon of gods and goddesses. The relationship between the creator and the created can vary from being separate and distinct to an intrinsic part of all that exists.

The concept of the creator has played a significant role in shaping human culture, morality, and ethics. It has been the source of inspiration for many works of art, literature, and music. It has also been a driving force behind the development of many ethical and moral systems.

In many cultures, the concept of the creator is intimately tied to the idea of creation and the origin of the world. The creation stories of various cultures often involve the actions of the creator, who is responsible for bringing the world into existence. These stories are often told as a way of explaining the meaning of life and providing a framework for how people should live.

The significance of the creator in various cultures and belief systems cannot be overstated. For many believers, the concept of the creator offers a sense of comfort, hope, and purpose, as they believe that they are part of a larger cosmic plan and that their lives have meaning and significance. The idea of a creator can also provide a sense of community and belonging, as people who share a belief in the creator often come together to worship and celebrate.

However, the concept of the creator has also been a source of controversy and conflict throughout history. Different religions and spiritual traditions have different ideas about the nature and attributes of the creator, leading to disputes and disagreements. Some people reject the concept of the creator altogether, seeing it as a relic of an outdated and superstitious worldview.

In conclusion, the concept of the creator is a central idea in many cultures and belief systems worldwide. It has been the source of inspiration, hope, and comfort for countless people throughout history, while also being the subject of debate and controversy. Its significance in shaping human culture and spirituality is undeniable, and it will continue to play an important role in the lives of believers and non-believers alike.

Scientific Theories of the Origin of the Universe

There are several scientific theories about the origin of the universe, each with its evidence and limitations. The two most prominent theories are the Big Bang Theory and the Steady State Theory. Let's explore these theories in more detail.

- The Big Bang Theory: This theory states that the universe began as a singular, incredibly hot and dense point, about 13.8 billion years ago. It then underwent rapid expansion, known as inflation, which caused it to cool and expand further. The universe is still expanding today, and the evidence for this includes cosmic microwave background radiation, which is the radiation leftover from the Big Bang.

The Big Bang Theory also explains the abundance of light elements like hydrogen and helium in the universe. The process of nucleosynthesis, which involves the fusion of these elements, occurred during the first few minutes of the universe's existence.

However, there are still some unanswered questions in the Big Bang Theory. For example, it cannot explain why the universe is structured the way it is, with galaxies and clusters of galaxies forming. There is also a discrepancy in the measurements of the Hubble constant, which is the rate at which the universe is expanding.

- The Steady State Theory: This theory states that the universe has no beginning or end and has always existed. It proposes that new matter is continuously created to maintain a constant density and expansion rate of the universe. This theory was proposed as an alternative to the Big Bang Theory in the 1940s and 50s.

However, the Steady State Theory has been largely discredited due to the lack of evidence to support it. The discovery of the cosmic microwave background radiation provided strong evidence for the Big Bang Theory, as it showed that the universe was once in a hot and dense state, which is consistent with the Big Bang.

Another theory that has gained traction in recent years is the inflationary theory. This theory proposes that the universe underwent an extremely rapid expansion in the first fraction of a second after the Big Bang. This theory helps to explain some of the inconsistencies in the Big Bang Theory, such as the structure of the universe.

In conclusion, the scientific theories of the origin of the universe continue to evolve as new evidence is discovered. While the Big Bang Theory is currently the most widely accepted, there are still some unanswered questions that scientists are working to address. As our understanding of the universe continues to grow, we can expect that our theories about its origin will continue to evolve as well.

Overview of the Big Bang Theory and other scientific theories explaining the origin of the universe

The Big Bang Theory is the most widely accepted scientific theory about the origin of the universe. It states that the universe began as a singular, incredibly hot and dense point, about 13.8 billion years ago. This point, which is often referred to as a singularity, underwent rapid expansion, known as inflation, which caused it to cool and expand further. The universe is still expanding today, and the evidence for this includes cosmic microwave background radiation, which is the radiation leftover from the Big Bang.

The Big Bang Theory also explains the abundance of light elements like hydrogen and helium in the universe. The process of nucleosynthesis, which involves the fusion of these elements, occurred during the first few minutes of the universe's existence.

Another scientific theory about the origin of the universe is the Steady State Theory. This theory states that the universe has no beginning or end and has always existed. It proposes that new matter is continuously created to maintain a constant density and expansion rate of the universe. However, this theory has been largely discredited due to the lack of evidence to support it. The inflationary theory has gained traction. This theory proposes that the universe underwent an extremely rapid expansion in the first fraction of a second after the Big Bang. This theory helps to explain some of the inconsistencies in the Big Bang Theory, such as the structure of the universe.

Other scientific theories about the origin of the universe include the cyclic universe theory, which proposes that the universe goes through cycles of expansion and contraction, and the string theory, which proposes that the universe is made up of tiny, vibrating strings.

The Big Bang Theory is the most widely accepted scientific theory about the origin of the universe, and it is supported by various lines of evidence. However, other scientific theories also exist, and scientists continue to explore and refine our understanding of the universe's origins.

Exploration of the limitations and uncertainties of scientific knowledge on this topic

Despite the significant progress that has been made in understanding the origins of the universe, there are still many uncertainties and limitations to our scientific knowledge on this topic.

One of the biggest limitations is the fact that we cannot directly observe the early universe. We can only study it indirectly through cosmic microwave background radiation, which is the radiation leftover from the Big Bang. While this radiation provides us with valuable information about the early universe, there are still many unanswered questions about what happened during the first few moments after the Big Bang.

Additionally, there are still some unanswered questions in the Big Bang Theory. For example, it cannot explain why the universe is structured the way it is, with galaxies and clusters of galaxies forming. There is also a discrepancy in the measurements of the Hubble constant, which is the rate at which the universe is expanding. This discrepancy suggests that there may be something fundamental about the universe that we still do not understand.

Another limitation is the fact that our current theories about the origins of the universe do not account for everything that we observe in the universe. For example, the presence of dark matter and dark energy, which together make up about 95% of the universe, cannot be explained by our current theories. While scientists have proposed various theories about the nature of dark matter and dark energy, these theories are still not fully understood.

In addition to these limitations, there are also uncertainties in our scientific knowledge about the origins of the universe. For example, the inflationary theory, which proposes that the universe underwent an extremely rapid expansion in the first fraction of a second after the Big Bang, is still a subject of debate among scientists. While there is evidence to support this theory, there are still many unanswered questions about how inflation occurred and what caused it.

while we have made significant progress in understanding the origins of the universe, there are still many uncertainties and limitations to our scientific knowledge on this topic. As our understanding of the universe continues to grow, we can expect that our theories about its origin will continue to evolve as well.

Religious and Philosophical Views on the Creator

Religious and philosophical views on the creator vary widely across different cultures and belief systems. Here are some examples:

- Monotheistic Religions: Many of the world's major religions, such as Judaism, Christianity, and Islam, believe in a single, all-powerful creator God who is responsible for the creation of the universe and all living things.

- Polytheistic Religions: Other religions, such as Hinduism and ancient Greek and Roman religions, believe in multiple gods who were responsible for the creation of the universe and who continue to play an active role in the world.

- Deism: Deism is a philosophical belief that posits the existence of a creator God who does not intervene in the world or human affairs. Deists believe that God created the universe and established the laws of nature but does not intervene in the course of events.

- Pantheism: Pantheism is the belief that the universe itself is divine and that the creator is synonymous with the universe. In this view, God is not a separate being but rather the total of all existence.

- Atheism: Atheism is the lack of belief in any deity or creator. Atheists do not believe that a God or gods created the universe or play any role in its functioning.

These are just a few examples of the many religious and philosophical views on the creator. Each belief system has its unique perspective on the nature of the creator and its relationship to the universe and humanity.

Examination of different religious and philosophical views on the concept of the creator, including the beliefs of Christianity, Islam, Judaism, Hinduism, Buddhism, and others

Here is an overview of different religious and philosophical views on the concept of the creator:

- Christianity: Christianity believes in one God who is the creator of the universe and all living things. God is often described as a loving father who is involved in the lives of his children. Christians believe that God created humans in his image and that he has a plan for each person's life.
- Islam: Islam also believes in one God who is the creator of the universe and all living things. God is often described as merciful and just, and Muslims believe that God's will is expressed through the Quran. Muslims believe that humans were created to worship God and to follow his laws.
- Judaism: Judaism also believes in one God who is the creator of the universe and all living things. God is often described as loving and just, and Jews believe that God made a covenant with the Jewish people to be his chosen people. Jews believe that humans were created to serve God and to follow his commandments.

- Hinduism: Hinduism believes in multiple gods who are responsible for the creation of the universe and who continue to play an active role in the world. Hindus believe that everything in the universe is interconnected and that the ultimate goal of life is to achieve moksha, or liberation from the cycle of birth and death.
- Buddhism: Buddhism does not believe in a creator God but rather in a universal energy or consciousness that permeates all things. Buddhists believe that suffering is caused by attachment to material things and that the ultimate goal of life is to achieve enlightenment and liberation from the cycle of suffering.
- Taoism: Taoism believes in a universal force called the Tao, which is responsible for the creation of the universe and all living things. Taoists believe that everything in the universe is interconnected and that the ultimate goal of life is to achieve harmony with the Tao.
- Deism: Deism is a philosophical belief that posits the existence of a creator God who does not intervene in the world or human affairs. Deists believe that God created the universe and established the laws of nature but does not intervene in the course of events.

These are just a few cxamples of the many religious and philosophical views on the concept of the creator. Each belief system has its unique perspective on the nature of the creator and its relationship to the universe and humanity.

Comparison of similarities and differences between various views

The views on the creator can vary widely depending on cultural, religious, and philosophical beliefs. Here is a comparison of some of the similarities and differences between various views on the creator:

Monotheistic views: Monotheistic religions such as Judaism, Christianity, and Islam believe in the existence of one God who is the creator of the universe. They also believe in the divine nature of God, his omniscience, omnipotence, and omnipresence.
Similarities: The belief in the existence of one God who is the creator of the universe is the common thread that binds monotheistic religions together.
Differences: The nature and attributes of God, the role of prophets, the concept of salvation, and the interpretation of holy texts are some of the areas where monotheistic religions differ.

Polytheistic views: Polytheistic religions believe in the existence of multiple gods and goddesses who are responsible for different aspects of the universe. Examples of polytheistic religions include Hinduism and ancient Greek and Roman religions.

Similarities: Polytheistic religions believe in the existence of multiple deities.
Differences: The nature and number of deities, the concept of creation, and the relationship between deities and humans are some of the areas where polytheistic religions differ.

Deistic views: Deism is the belief in the existence of a creator who created the universe but does not intervene in its affairs. Deists believe that the creator set the universe in motion but does not interfere with its workings.

Similarities: The belief in a creator who created the universe is the common thread that binds deistic views together.
Differences: Deistic views differ from other religious views in that they do not believe in the divine nature of the creator, and they reject the notion of divine intervention in human affairs.

Pantheistic views: Pantheistic beliefs hold that everything in the universe is divine and that the universe itself is God. In pantheism, God and the universe are the same.
Similarities: Pantheistic views see divinity in everything and believe in the interconnectedness of all things.
Differences: Pantheistic views differ from other religious views in that they do not believe in a personal God who intervenes in human affairs.

Atheistic views: Atheism is the lack of belief in the existence of a God or gods. Atheists do not believe in a creator or supernatural beings.
Similarities: Atheistic views reject the existence of a creator or supernatural beings
Differences: Atheistic views differ from other religious views in that they do not believe in the existence of a divine being or beings.

The Problem of Evil

The Problem of Evil is a philosophical and theological issue that arises from the existence of evil and suffering in the world. It raises the question of how the existence of evil and suffering can be reconciled with the existence of an all-powerful, all-knowing, and all-loving God.

The problem can be stated in the following way: If God is all-powerful, he could prevent evil and suffering from existing. If God is all-knowing, he would know about the evil and suffering that exists. If God is all-loving, he would want to prevent evil and suffering from existing. However, evil and suffering do exist, so either God is not all-powerful, not all-knowing, or not all-loving, or he does not exist at all.

The problem of evil can be approached from different perspectives. One response to the problem is theodicy, which is the attempt to reconcile the existence of evil with the existence of an all-powerful, all-knowing, and all-loving God. Theodicies come in different forms and often rely on theological or philosophical arguments.

Another response to the problem of evil is the rejection of one or more of the assumptions that lead to the problem. For example, some argue that God is not all-powerful or all-knowing, or that God's love is not the same as human love, and therefore, evil and suffering can coexist with an all-powerful and all-loving God.

The problem of evil remains one of the most difficult challenges to religious belief and has been debated by philosophers and theologians for centuries. It is a complex issue that requires careful consideration of different arguments and perspectives.

Discussion of the philosophical problem of evil and how it relates to the concept of the creator

The philosophical problem of evil is one of the most difficult challenges to the belief in an all-powerful, all-knowing, and all-loving creator. The problem arises from the existence of evil and suffering in the world, which seems incompatible with the existence of a perfect and benevolent creator.

The problem of evil has been the subject of philosophical and theological inquiry for centuries. The problem is typically framed as a logical argument, which goes something like this:

- If God is all-powerful, he can prevent evil and suffering from existing.
- If God is all-knowing, he knows about the evil and suffering that exists.
- If God is all-loving, he would want to prevent evil and suffering from existing.
- Evil and suffering exist in the world.
- Therefore, either God is not all-powerful, not all-knowing, or not all-loving, or he does not exist at all.

One way to approach the problem of evil is to deny one or more of the assumptions that lead to the conclusion of the argument. For example, some argue that God is not all-powerful or all-knowing, and therefore cannot prevent evil and suffering from existing. Others argue that God's love is not the same as human love, and that what appears to us as evil and suffering may be part of a larger, unknown plan that is ultimately good.

Another way to approach the problem is to argue that evil and suffering are necessary for certain goods, such as moral growth, free will, or the ability to appreciate the good. This is known as theodicy, which is the attempt to reconcile the existence of evil with the existence of an all-powerful, all-knowing, and all-loving God.

However, these responses to the problem of evil do not provide a definitive solution to the problem. The problem remains a profound challenge to the belief in an all-powerful and benevolent creator, and it raises deep questions about the nature of God, the nature of evil, and the purpose of human life.

The problem of evil is a philosophical challenge to the belief in an all-powerful, all-knowing, and all-loving creator. It raises profound questions about the nature of God and the nature of evil, and it remains a difficult issue to resolve. Philosophers and theologians continue to debate the problem of evil, seeking answers consistent with religious belief and human experience.

Examination of various attempts to reconcile the existence of a benevolent creator with the existence of evil and suffering in the world

There have been various attempts to reconcile the existence of a benevolent creator with the existence of evil and suffering in the world. Some of the most significant attempts are discussed below:

- Free Will Defence: One common response to the problem of evil is the Free Will Defense. This argument suggests that God created humans with free will, which includes the ability to choose between good and evil. Therefore, it is not God's responsibility to prevent evil and suffering, but rather humans are responsible for their actions. According to this view, God created the world in such a way that humans have the freedom to choose, and with that freedom comes the possibility of evil and suffering.
- Theodicy of Soul-Making: Another response to the problem of evil is the theodicy of soul-making, which suggests that evil and suffering are necessary for human moral and spiritual development. This view posits that humans are not born morally perfect but must develop their character through experiences that challenge them. Thus, the existence of evil and suffering can help humans develop their character and become morally better people.
- Privation Theory: The privation theory suggests that evil is not a positive entity but rather a privation or lack of good. According to this view, evil is not a thing that exists but rather the absence of good. Therefore, God did not create evil, but rather it is a result of the absence

of good.

- Greater Good Defense: The greater good defence argues that God allows evil and suffering in the world because it ultimately serves a greater good. This view suggests that the existence of evil can be justified if it leads to a greater good in the long run, such as the growth of human character or the attainment of greater moral or spiritual goods.
- Mystery Defense: Finally, some philosophers and theologians argue that the problem of evil is ultimately a mystery that we cannot fully understand. According to this view, God's ways are beyond our comprehension, and the existence of evil and suffering is a mystery that we cannot fully explain.

There have been various attempts to reconcile the existence of a benevolent creator with the existence of evil and suffering in the world. These attempts range from the Free Will Defense to the Mystery Defense. While none of these responses provides a definitive solution to the problem, they illustrate the ongoing philosophical and theological debate surrounding the issue.

The Role of Free Will

Free will is the ability to make choices that are not determined by external factors or prior causes. It is the power to act freely and independently, based on our desires, beliefs, and values. In the context of religion and philosophy, free will is often seen as a crucial aspect of human existence, allowing us to make moral choices, take responsibility for our actions, and develop our character.

The concept of free will plays a significant role in many religious and philosophical discussions, particularly when it comes to questions of morality and the nature of the human soul. In many religions, free will is seen as a gift from God, allowing humans to choose between good and evil, and to be responsible for their actions. According to this view, humans can choose to do what is right, even in the face of adversity or temptation.

In philosophy, free will is often seen as a necessary condition for moral responsibility. If our actions are determined by external factors or prior causes, then it would seem that we are not fully responsible for our actions. However, if we have the power to choose freely, then we can be held accountable for our choices, and we can be praised or blamed accordingly.

The concept of free will also plays a significant role in debates surrounding the problem of evil. One common response to the problem is the Free Will Defense, which suggests that God created humans with free will, allowing them to choose between good and evil. According to this view, the existence of evil is not the result of God's actions, but rather the actions of humans who choose to do evil.

The concept of free will is a central aspect of religious and philosophical discussions surrounding morality, responsibility, and the nature of human existence. While the role of free will in shaping our lives is complex and often debated, it is clear that our ability to choose freely plays a significant role in our sense of moral responsibility and our capacity for moral growth.

Exploration of the role of free will in various views of the creator and its significance in the problem of evil

The role of free will is an important aspect of many views of the creator and the problem of evil. Here are some examples:

- Theism: Many theistic religions, such as Christianity, Islam, and Judaism, posit the existence of a benevolent and all-powerful creator who gave humans free will. According to this view, God created humans with the ability to choose between good and evil and to be responsible for their actions. Therefore, the existence of evil and suffering is not due to God's actions, but rather the result of human choices.
- In the problem of evil, the role of free will is often used to explain the existence of evil in the world. The Free Will Defense argues that God allows evil to exist in the world because humans have free will, and the ability to choose between good and evil. Therefore, it is not God's responsibility to prevent evil and suffering, but rather humans are responsible for their actions.

- Deism: Deism is the belief that a creator god exists, but that this god is not involved in the affairs of the world. According to this view, the creator set the universe in motion but does not intervene in the world or interact with humans. In the context of free will, deism suggests that the creator gave humans free will, but does not intervene to prevent the consequences of their actions.
- In the problem of evil, deism suggests that the creator is not responsible for the existence of evil and suffering, but rather humans are responsible for their actions. However, it does not offer a solution to the problem, as it does not explain why a benevolent creator would create a world where evil and suffering exist.
- Pantheism: Pantheism is the belief that the universe and everything in it is God. In this view, there is no separation between the creator and the created; everything is connected. In the context of free will, pantheism suggests that humans have free will because they are a part of God.

In the problem of evil, pantheism suggests that humans can choose between good and evil because they are a part of God. Therefore, the existence of evil and suffering is the result of human choices, but it is also a part of the natural order of the universe.

The role of free will is significant in many views of the creator and the problem of evil. While the exact relationship between free will, the creator, and the existence of evil is complex and often debated, it is clear that the concept of free will is central to our understanding of moral responsibility and the nature of human existence.

Examination of different interpretations of free will and its relationship with the concept of a creator

Free will is a concept that is open to various interpretations in different philosophical and religious traditions. Here are some examples of different interpretations of free will and their relationship with the concept of a creator:

- Libertarianism: In the context of free will, libertarianism suggests that humans can make choices that are not determined by prior causes or external factors. According to this view, free will is incompatible with determinism, which posits that all events, including human actions, are determined by prior causes.
  In the context of a creator, libertarianism suggests that the creator gave humans free will as a gift, allowing them to choose between good and evil. According to this view, the creator is not responsible for human actions, but rather humans are responsible for their choices.
- Compatibilism: Compatibilism is the view that free will is compatible with determinism. According to this view, humans can make choices that are determined by prior causes, but they still have free will because they are making those choices based on their desires and beliefs.
  In the context of a creator, compatibilism suggests that the creator gave humans free will, but that free will is compatible with the creator's ultimate plan. According to this view, the creator is responsible for the natural order of the universe, including the existence of evil and suffering, but humans still can make choices within that order.

- Hard Determinism: Hard determinism is the view that free will is an illusion and that all events, including human actions, are determined by prior causes. According to this view, humans cannot make choices that are not determined by external factors. In the context of a creator, hard determinism suggests that the creator is responsible for everything that happens in the universe, including human actions. According to this view, the creator is responsible for the existence of evil and suffering, and humans cannot be held morally responsible for their actions.
- Fatalism: Fatalism is the view that all events, including human actions, are predetermined and cannot be changed. According to this view, humans cannot make choices that can alter the course of events. In the context of a creator, fatalism suggests that the creator has predetermined everything that happens in the universe, including human actions. According to this view, humans do not have free will, and the existence of evil and suffering is ultimately the responsibility of the creator.

The relationship between free will and the concept of a creator is complex and open to various interpretations. While some views suggest that the creator gave humans free will as a gift, others suggest that free will is an illusion, or that everything is predetermined by the creator. These different interpretations have significant implications for questions of morality, responsibility, and the problem of evil.

Contemporary Debates on the Creator

Several contemporary debates on the creator are ongoing in philosophical and religious circles. Here are some examples of these debates:

- Intelligent Design vs. Evolution: This debate concerns the origin of life and the universe. Proponents of intelligent design argue that the complexity of living organisms and the universe cannot be explained by natural processes alone, and must have been designed by a creator. On the other hand, proponents of evolution argue that the complexity of life can be explained by natural selection and random mutation and that there is no need to invoke a creator to explain the origins of life and the universe.
- The Problem of Evil: The problem of evil is a long-standing philosophical and religious debate about the existence of evil and suffering in the world, and how it relates to the concept of a benevolent creator. Some argue that the existence of evil and suffering is evidence against the existence of a benevolent creator, while others argue that there are ways to reconcile the existence of evil and suffering with the concept of a benevolent creator.
- The Concept of God in the Modern World: This debate concerns the relevance of the concept of a creator in the modern world. Some argue that the concept of a creator is outdated and irrelevant in a scientific and secular world, while others argue that the concept of a creator still has value as a source of morality, meaning, and purpose.

- Atheism vs. Theism: This debate concerns the existence of a creator or god. Atheists argue that there is no evidence for the existence of a creator or god, while theists argue that there is evidence for the existence of a creator or god through religious experiences, arguments from design, and other philosophical and theological arguments.
- Religious Pluralism: This debate concerns the relationship between different religious traditions and their conceptions of the creator. Some argue that there is only one true religion or one true conception of the creator, while others argue that there are multiple valid religious traditions and conceptions of the creator.

These debates continue to be the subject of ongoing research and discussion in philosophical and religious circles and have important implications for our understanding of the nature of the universe and our place in it.

Overview of contemporary debates on the concept of the creator, including scientific, philosophical, and theological debates

Contemporary debates on the concept of the creator cover a range of topics and involve scientific, philosophical, and theological discussions. Here is an overview of some of the key debates:

- Scientific Debates: There are ongoing debates within scientific circles regarding the origins of the universe and life, and whether the concept of a creator is compatible with scientific explanations. The debate between intelligent design and evolution is one example of this. Some scientists argue that the complexity of living organisms and the universe points to the existence of a creator, while others argue that scientific evidence supports the theory of evolution and natural selection as an explanation for the origins of life.

- Philosophical Debates: The philosophical debate on the creator centres on issues such as the problem of evil, the nature of free will, and the role of the creator in ethical and moral considerations. The problem of evil raises the question of how a benevolent creator can allow for the existence of evil and suffering in the world. The nature of free will is another philosophical debate, which considers the compatibility of free will and the existence of a creator who is omniscient and omnipotent. Additionally, the role of the creator in ethical and moral considerations raises questions about the relationship between the creator and moral principles.
- Theological Debates: Theological debates on the creator centre on questions of faith and religious doctrine. There are debates on the nature of the creator, the relationship between the creator and human beings, and the role of the creator in religious traditions. Additionally, there are debates on the interpretation of religious texts and the extent to which these texts guide the nature of the creator and the relationship between the creator and human beings.
- Interfaith Debates: Interfaith debates on the creator focus on the different conceptions of the creator within various religious traditions. There are debates on the

relationship between monotheistic and polytheistic traditions, as well as debates on the relationship between different monotheistic traditions. Additionally, there are debates on the extent to which different religious traditions offer a coherent understanding of the nature of the creator.

Contemporary debates on the concept of the creator involve a range of perspectives and disciplines and are ongoing discussions in scientific, philosophical, theological, and interfaith contexts.

Discussion of recent developments and new ideas in this field

Recent developments and new ideas in the field of the creator have focused on bridging the gap between science and religion, exploring new conceptions of the creator, and re-examining traditional theological and philosophical ideas. Here are some examples:

- The Emergence of Science-Religion Dialogue: One recent development in the field is the emergence of science-religion dialogue, which seeks to bridge the gap between scientific and religious perspectives on the universe and its origins. This dialogue aims to explore ways in which science and religion can complement each other in understanding the universe and our place in it.
- New Conceptions of the Creator: Another recent development is the exploration of new conceptions of the creator, which challenge traditional understandings

of the creator. Some scholars have proposed a pantheistic view of the creator, which sees the universe itself as the divine, while others have proposed a process theology view, which sees the creator as constantly evolving and changing in response to the world.

- Re-Examination of Traditional Ideas: A third recent development is the re-examination of traditional theological and philosophical ideas about the creator. For example, some scholars have challenged the traditional idea of divine omnipotence, arguing that it limits the freedom and responsibility of human beings. Others have explored the idea of a non-interventionist creator, which allows for free will and natural processes to unfold without divine intervention.
- Interfaith Dialogue: Finally, there has been an increased focus on interfaith dialogue, which seeks to understand the different conceptions of the creator within different religious traditions. Interfaith dialogue aims to promote mutual understanding and respect, while also identifying commonalities and differences in religious views of the creator.

Recent developments and new ideas in the field of the creator reflect a growing interest in exploring new perspectives and approaches to understanding the nature of the universe and our relationship with the divine. These developments offer new insights and challenges to traditional theological and philosophical ideas and provide opportunities for interdisciplinary dialogue and collaboration.

Implications of the Concept of the Creator

The concept of the creator has far-reaching implications for our understanding of the universe and our place in it. Whether through religious, philosophical, or scientific perspectives, the idea of a creator raises important questions about the nature of existence, morality, and purpose.

From a religious standpoint, the concept of the creator provides a foundation for faith and belief, offering guidance and inspiration for individuals and communities. It also raises questions about the relationship between the divine and human beings and the role of religion in shaping human values and behaviour.

From a philosophical standpoint, the concept of the creator raises fundamental questions about the nature of reality, the existence of evil and suffering, and the role of free will in human life. Philosophical debates about the creator have led to important insights into ethics, morality, and the meaning of life.

From a scientific standpoint, the concept of the creator has led to ongoing debates about the origins of the universe and the nature of life. Scientific investigations into the nature of the universe and its origins have shed light on our understanding of the world, while also challenging traditional religious beliefs.

The concept of the creator continues to be a source of fascination and inquiry, inviting ongoing dialogue and exploration across multiple fields and disciplines. While there are many different perspectives on the nature of the creator, the implications of this concept remain significant for our understanding of the world and our place in it.

Reflection on the significance and implications of the concept of the creator for different aspects of human life and society.

The concept of the creator has significant implications for different aspects of human life and society. Here are some reflections:

- Ethics and Morality: The concept of the creator has been a major influence on ethics and morality throughout human history. It provides a foundation for many religious and philosophical systems of morality and informs our understanding of what is right and wrong. The idea of a creator also raises important questions about the nature of good and evil and the role of free will in moral decision-making.
- Religion and Spirituality: The concept of the creator is central to many religious and spiritual traditions, providing a framework for faith and belief. The idea of a creator offers a sense of purpose, meaning, and direction to individuals and communities, and shapes religious practices, rituals, and beliefs.
- Science and Philosophy: The concept of the creator has also been a subject of inquiry for scientists and philosophers, leading to new insights into the nature of reality, the origins of the universe, and the role of human beings in the cosmos. It has also led to important debates about the relationship between science and

religion, and the compatibility of scientific and religious perspectives.

- Politics and Society: The concept of the creator has also had a significant impact on politics and society, shaping laws, institutions, and cultural norms. It has informed our understanding of human rights, social justice, and the role of government in promoting the common good. It has also been a source of conflict and division, leading to debates about the relationship between religion and state, and the appropriate role of religious beliefs in public life.

The concept of the creator has profound implications for different aspects of human life and society, including ethics and morality, religion and spirituality, science and philosophy, and politics and society. While there are many different perspectives on the nature of the creator, the implications of this concept continue to shape our understanding of the world and our place in it.

CHAPTER FOUR

Principles of Good Governance

Good governance refers to the process of managing and directing public affairs in a way that is accountable, transparent, participatory, responsive, effective, equitable, and inclusive. It is essential for creating and maintaining a stable and prosperous society, promoting economic growth, reducing poverty, ensuring social justice, protecting human rights, and preserving the environment.

Good governance matters because it creates an environment where citizens can trust their leaders and institutions, where there is a level playing field for all stakeholders, and where public resources are used efficiently and effectively. It fosters a culture of collaboration, dialogue, and consensus-building, which is critical for addressing complex challenges and achieving sustainable development.

The key principles and values that underpin good governance include:

- Accountability: This refers to the obligation of those in power to justify their decisions and actions, and to be held responsible for their performance.
- Transparency: This means ensuring that information is accessible to the public and that decisions and actions are open to scrutiny.
- Participation: This involves involving citizens and stakeholders in decision-making processes, and ensuring that their voices are heard and taken into account.
- Responsiveness: This refers to the ability of leaders and institutions to respond to the needs and concerns of citizens and stakeholders.
- Effectiveness: This means ensuring that policies and programs are implemented efficiently and that they achieve their intended outcomes.
- Equity: This involves ensuring that all citizens have equal access to opportunities and resources and that there is no discrimination or favouritism.
- Inclusiveness: This means ensuring that all segments of society are represented and have a voice in decision-making processes, regardless of their social, economic, or political status.

Good governance is critical for creating a stable, prosperous, and just society, and for achieving sustainable development.

Transparency and Accountability:

Transparency and accountability are fundamental principles of good governance. Transparency refers to the openness of government institutions, processes, and information to public scrutiny, while accountability refers to the obligation of those in power to justify their decisions and actions and to be held responsible for their performance. Here are some examples of how these principles can be put into practice in various contexts:

- Public finances: Governments can promote transparency by publishing budgetary information, including revenue and expenditure figures, in a clear and accessible manner. They can also establish independent bodies, such as auditors or ombudsmen, to oversee and scrutinize public finances, and ensure that public funds are used effectively and efficiently.
- Elections: To promote transparency and accountability in electoral processes, governments can establish independent electoral commissions, publish election laws and procedures, and provide access to voter registration information. They can also encourage media and civil society organizations to monitor and report on election processes.
- Public procurement: Governments can promote transparency and accountability in public procurement processes by ensuring that procurement laws and procedures are clear and publicly available. They can also establish independent oversight bodies to monitor procurement processes, publish procurement contracts, and ensure that procurement decisions are fair, open, and competitive.

- Freedom of information: Governments can promote transparency by guaranteeing the right of citizens to access information held by government institutions. They can establish laws and procedures that make it easy for citizens to access information, and provide training and support to public officials to ensure that they respond to requests for information in a timely and accurate manner.
- Corporate governance: Transparency and accountability are also important in the private sector. Companies can promote transparency by publishing financial statements and annual reports, disclosing information about their ownership structure, and establishing independent oversight bodies, such as audit committees or boards of directors, to monitor and report on company performance.

Transparency and accountability are essential principles of good governance, and their application is critical in ensuring that public institutions and private companies are open, honest, and accountable to their stakeholders. By promoting transparency and accountability in these various contexts, governments and businesses can build trust with their citizens and customers, and contribute to the achievement of sustainable development goals.

Rule of Law

The rule of law is a cornerstone of good governance, and explore different dimensions of this concept such as legal certainty, access to justice, and the role of courts and other legal institutions.

The rule of law is a fundamental principle of good

governance that ensures that all individuals, including government officials, are subject to the law and are held accountable for their actions. It establishes a framework of legal certainty that provides stability, predictability, and protection of human rights. Here are some key dimensions of the rule of law and their importance in good governance:

- Legal certainty: This refers to the predictability and clarity of the law. Laws must be clear and accessible to all individuals, and their application must be consistent and transparent. Legal certainty is essential for creating a stable and predictable environment for economic and social activity, as well as for protecting human rights.
- Access to justice: This refers to the ability of individuals to seek and obtain justice through the legal system. It is essential that the legal system is accessible, impartial, and independent, and that all individuals have equal access to justice, regardless of their social, economic, or political status. Access to justice is critical for protecting human rights, resolving disputes, and maintaining the rule of law.
- Role of courts and legal institutions: Courts and other legal institutions play a critical role in upholding the rule of law. They must be independent, impartial, and effective in enforcing the law and resolving disputes. It is essential that they are adequately resourced and staffed, and that they are accessible to all individuals. The role of courts and legal institutions is essential in protecting the rights of citizens, ensuring compliance with the law, and promoting legal certainty.

In practice, the rule of law can be strengthened through a range of measures, including the establishment of strong and independent legal institutions, the training of legal professionals, the provision of legal aid to those who cannot afford it, and the development of effective mechanisms for accountability and oversight. It is also important to ensure that the law is consistent with international human rights standards and that it is enforced in a manner that protects the rights of all individuals.

The rule of law is a cornerstone of good governance, ensuring legal certainty, access to justice, and the proper functioning of legal institutions. Its effective implementation is critical for promoting economic growth, protecting human rights, and ensuring a stable and just society.

Participation and Civic Engagement

Importance of citizen participation and civic engagement in good governance, and discuss different ways in which people can be involved in decision-making processes at various levels.

Citizen participation and civic engagement are crucial components of good governance, as they promote accountability, transparency, and legitimacy in decision-making processes. By involving citizens in the decision-making process, governments can ensure that policies are more responsive to the needs and aspirations of the people they serve. Here are some ways in which people can be involved in decision-making processes at various levels:

- Consultation: Governments can consult with citizens on specific issues or policies by seeking their input through public hearings, surveys, or online platforms. This can help ensure that policies are more responsive to the needs and aspirations of the people they serve, and can help build trust between citizens and government.
- Participation in governance structures: Citizens can be involved in decision-making processes by serving on committees or task forces that advise government officials on specific issues or policies. This allows citizens to provide input and expertise and can help ensure that policies are more responsive to the needs of the community.
- Community organizing: Citizens can organize themselves into groups or associations to advocate for their interests and priorities. This can help ensure that policies are more responsive to the needs and priorities of the community, and can help build social cohesion and resilience.
- Public service: Citizens can also participate in decision-making processes by serving in public office, running for elected positions, or working in government agencies. This can help ensure that policies are more responsive to the needs of the community, and can help build trust between citizens and government.
- Citizen monitoring: Citizens can monitor the implementation of policies and projects to ensure that they are being implemented effectively and efficiently. This can help promote accountability and transparency and can help identify areas for improvement.

Citizen participation and civic engagement are critical components of good governance. By involving citizens in decision-making processes, governments can ensure that policies are more responsive to the needs and aspirations of the people they serve, and can help build trust and legitimacy. Citizens can be involved in decision-making processes in a range of ways, from consultation to public service, and governments must create opportunities for meaningful engagement and participation.

Responsiveness and Responsiveness:

Importance of responsiveness and responsiveness in good governance, and discuss different strategies for ensuring that governments and other institutions can respond to the needs and preferences of the people they serve.

Responsiveness and accountability are critical components of good governance, as they ensure that governments and other institutions can respond to the needs and preferences of the people they serve. Here are some strategies for ensuring that governments and other institutions are responsive and accountable:

- Feedback mechanisms: Governments can establish feedback mechanisms, such as hotlines or suggestion boxes, that allow citizens to provide input and feedback on policies and services. This can help ensure that policies are more responsive to the needs and preferences of the community, and can help identify areas for improvement.
- Open data and transparency: Governments can make data and information about policies and services

available to the public. This can help build trust and legitimacy and can help identify areas for improvement.

- Performance-based budgeting: Governments can use performance-based budgeting to allocate resources based on outcomes and results rather than inputs. This can help ensure that resources are allocated in a way that is more responsive to the needs and preferences of the community.
- Citizen participation: As mentioned earlier, citizen participation is a critical component of good governance. Governments can involve citizens in decision-making processes to ensure that policies are more responsive to the needs and preferences of the community.
- Monitoring and evaluation: Governments can establish monitoring and evaluation mechanisms to assess the effectiveness of policies and services. This can help identify areas for improvement and ensure that policies are more responsive to the needs and preferences of the community.
- Responsive service delivery: Governments can ensure that services are delivered in a timely, efficient, and effective manner. This can help ensure that policies are more responsive to the needs and preferences of the community, and can help build trust and legitimacy.

Responsiveness and accountability are critical components of good governance. Governments and other institutions can ensure that they are responsive and accountable by establishing feedback mechanisms, promoting transparency, using performance-based budgeting, involving citizens in decision-making processes, monitoring and evaluating policies and services, and ensuring that services are delivered in a timely and efficient manner. By doing so, they can ensure that policies are more responsive to the needs and preferences of the people they serve, and can help build trust and legitimacy.

Anti-Corruption and Ethics

Role of anti-corruption measures and ethical standards in good governance, and provide examples of how these principles can be applied in different contexts.

Anti-corruption measures and ethical standards are essential components of good governance. Corruption can undermine the legitimacy and effectiveness of government institutions and lead to widespread social and economic inequalities. Here are some examples of how these principles can be applied in different contexts in India:

- Transparency: One of the key anti-corruption measures is promoting transparency. India has implemented several measures to increase transparency in government operations, such as the Right to Information Act, which allows citizens to access government records and information. Additionally, the government has implemented digital platforms like e-procurement and e-tendering to increase transparency in government procurement processes.
- Whistleblower Protection: Another important anti-corruption measure is whistleblower protection. India has a Whistleblowers Protection Act that provides legal protection to whistleblowers who report corruption or other wrongdoings. This act has helped increase transparency and accountability in government operations.

- Code of Conduct and Ethics: Establishing a code of conduct and ethical standards for public officials is crucial in promoting good governance. In India, the Central Vigilance Commission (CVC) has developed a code of conduct and ethics for public officials to ensure that they maintain the highest ethical standards while performing their duties.
- Digitalization of services: Digitalization of services in India has helped to reduce corruption by minimizing human interaction and increasing transparency in government operations. For instance, the use of digital platforms for the delivery of government services has reduced the scope for corrupt practices such as bribes for providing services.
- Strong Anti-Corruption Laws: India has a range of laws to prevent and punish corruption, such as the Prevention of Corruption Act and the Benami Transactions (Prohibition) Act. The government has also set up agencies such as the Central Bureau of Investigation (CBI) and the Enforcement Directorate (ED) to investigate and prosecute cases of corruption and money laundering.

Anti-corruption measures and ethical standards are critical components of good governance. India has implemented several measures to promote transparency, establish codes of conduct and ethics, protect whistleblowers, digitize services, and enforce anti-corruption laws. These measures have helped to reduce corruption and promote good governance in the country. However, more efforts need to be made to address the challenges of corruption and ensure that ethical standards are maintained in government operations.

Public Sector Reform:

Challenges and opportunities associated with public sector reform, and discuss different strategies for improving the effectiveness and efficiency of government institutions.

Public sector reform is critical for improving the effectiveness and efficiency of government institutions. However, it is often a challenging process that involves significant political and institutional hurdles. Here are some challenges and opportunities associated with public sector reform in India, as well as strategies for improving the effectiveness and efficiency of government institutions:

Challenges:

- Political opposition: Public sector reform is often met with political opposition, particularly from interest groups and individuals who benefit from the status quo.
- Bureaucratic resistance: Government bureaucracy can be resistant to change, particularly if it involves reducing the size or scope of their operations.
- Resource constraints: Lack of resources, particularly financial resources, can limit the capacity of government institutions to implement public sector reforms.
- Lack of political will: Public sector reform requires strong political leadership and will, which may be lacking in some cases.

Opportunities:

- Technological advancements: Advancements in technology have made it easier to streamline government operations and reduce bureaucracy.
- Citizen demand: There is growing demand from citizens for better and more efficient government services, which can help drive public sector reform.
- International support: International organizations and donor agencies can provide support and resources to countries that are implementing public sector reform.

Strategies:

- Digitalization of services: Digitalization of government services can help reduce bureaucracy, increase transparency, and improve efficiency. For instance, the use of digital platforms for the delivery of government services can reduce the time and cost involved in providing services.
- Performance-based management: Government institutions can be made more effective and efficient by implementing performance-based management systems. This involves setting clear objectives, measuring performance, and rewarding or penalizing based on performance.
- Capacity building: Capacity building can help strengthen government institutions and equip them with the skills and resources needed to implement public sector reforms.
- Public-private partnerships: Public-private partnerships can help improve the effectiveness and efficiency of government institutions by leveraging private sector

expertise and resources.
- Regulatory reform: Regulatory reform can help reduce bureaucratic red tape, encourage entrepreneurship, and promote economic growth.

Public sector reform is critical for improving the effectiveness and efficiency of government institutions. Although there are challenges associated with public sector reform, there are also opportunities and strategies that can be employed to improve government operations. Digitalization of services, performance-based management, capacity building, public-private partnerships, and regulatory reform are some of the strategies that can help improve the effectiveness and efficiency of Indian government institutions.

Local Governance and Decentralization:

Importance of local governance and decentralization in good governance, and examine different models and approaches for devolving power and resources to the local level.

Local governance and decentralization are important components of good governance as they can promote greater citizen participation, improve service delivery, and enhance accountability. Decentralization involves the transfer of power and resources from the central government to local governments or other sub-national entities. Here are some models and approaches for devolving power and resources to the local level:

- Devolution of political power: This involves transferring decision-making power from the central government to local governments. This can be done through various means such as constitutional reforms, legal frameworks, or administrative processes. Devolution of political power can lead to greater citizen participation in decision-making processes and improve accountability.
- Fiscal decentralization: Fiscal decentralization involves the transfer of financial resources from the central government to local governments. This can be done through various means such as intergovernmental transfers, local taxation, or borrowing. Fiscal decentralization can help promote greater efficiency and effectiveness in service delivery as local governments are often better placed to understand the needs of their constituents.
- Delegation of administrative functions: This involves delegating administrative functions from the central government to local governments. This can be done through various means such as delegation of powers, delegation of functions, or delegation of personnel. Delegation of administrative functions can help improve the efficiency and effectiveness of service delivery by bringing decision-making closer to the point of service delivery.
- Participatory governance: Participatory governance involves the active participation of citizens in decision-making processes. This can be done through various means such as citizen participation in budgeting, participatory planning, or participatory monitoring and evaluation. Participatory governance can help promote greater citizen engagement and accountability in decision-making processes.

- Collaborative governance: Collaborative governance involves the collaboration between different levels of government, civil society organizations, and the private sector to address complex public policy challenges. This can be done through various means such as public-private partnerships, co-governance, or multi-stakeholder initiatives. Collaborative governance can help improve the effectiveness and efficiency of service delivery by leveraging the resources and expertise of different stakeholders.

Local governance and decentralization are important components of good governance as they can promote greater citizen participation, improve service delivery, and enhance accountability. Devolution of political power, fiscal decentralization, delegation of administrative functions, participatory governance, and collaborative governance are some of the models and approaches that can be used to devolve power and resources to the local level. It is important for governments to carefully consider the appropriate model and approach to use, based on their specific context and needs.

International Dimensions of Good Governance

International dimensions of good governance, including the role of international organizations, treaties and conventions, and other forms of global governance.

Good governance is not just a domestic concern but also has important international dimensions. Several international organizations, treaties, and conventions promote good governance and provide guidance and support to countries in this regard.

The United Nations (UN) plays a significant role in promoting good governance at the global level. The UN has developed several international frameworks, such as the Sustainable Development Goals (SDGs), which aim to promote sustainable development and good governance. The UN also supports capacity building and technical assistance to countries to improve their governance systems.

International financial institutions such as the World Bank and International Monetary Fund (IMF) also play an important role in promoting good governance. They provide loans and technical assistance to countries to strengthen their governance systems and promote transparency and accountability. These institutions often tie their financial support to specific governance reforms and performance indicators.

Several treaties and conventions also promote good governance at the international level. For example, the United Nations Convention Against Corruption (UNCAC) is a global treaty that aims to prevent, detect, and punish corruption. The Organisation for Economic Co-operation and Development (OECD) Anti-Bribery Convention is another example of an international agreement that aims to combat bribery and corruption in international business transactions.

In addition to these international organizations and treaties, other forms of global governance promote good governance. For example, civil society organizations, including international non-governmental organizations (NGOs), can play an important role in monitoring and advocating for good governance. Private sector initiatives, such as corporate social responsibility programs, can also promote good governance practices in the business sector.

Good governance is not only a domestic concern but also has important international dimensions. The role of international organizations, treaties and conventions, and other forms of global governance are essential for promoting and supporting good governance practices around the world. Countries should engage in these international frameworks and cooperate with international partners to improve their governance systems and promote sustainable development.

Future Directions

Summarizing the key themes and ideas covered, and looking ahead to future challenges and opportunities for promoting good governance around the world.

Throughout this discussion, we have explored the concept of good governance, its importance, and the key principles and values that underpin it. We have discussed the role of transparency and accountability, the rule of law, citizen participation, responsiveness, anti-corruption measures, and local governance in promoting good governance. We have also examined the international dimensions of good governance, including the role of international organizations, treaties and conventions, and other forms of global governance.

Looking ahead, there are several challenges and opportunities for promoting good governance around the world. These include addressing issues such as inequality, political polarization, and the erosion of democratic norms and institutions. It is also important to recognize the importance of context-specific solutions, as what works in one country may not necessarily work in another.

In addition, emerging technologies such as artificial intelligence, blockchain, and big data analytics have the potential to transform governance systems and promote greater transparency and accountability. However, these technologies also bring new challenges and risks that need to be carefully considered and managed.

Moreover, the COVID-19 pandemic has highlighted the importance of effective governance in addressing global challenges and the need for adaptive governance systems that can respond to crises in real time.

Promoting good governance is essential for ensuring sustainable development, protecting human rights, and building resilient societies. It requires sustained efforts and cooperation among various stakeholders, including governments, civil society organizations, the private sector, and international organizations. By working together, we can create a better future for all.

CHAPTER FIVE

Ram - Beyond a Religious Figure

Ram is indeed a significant figure in Hinduism, but he is much more than just a deity. Ram is a symbol of morality, ethics, and righteousness in Hindu culture. His story, as depicted in the Hindu epic Ramayana, has a profound impact on Indian society, shaping its beliefs, customs, and traditions.

The character of Ram is revered for his noble qualities, such as courage, truthfulness, compassion, and devotion to duty. His story teaches important lessons about morality, spirituality, and the importance of fulfilling one's duties in life. Ram's teachings have had a lasting influence on Indian culture, and they continue to inspire people to lead virtuous life.

Furthermore, Ram is also seen as a model ruler, and his reign is considered a golden age in Indian history. His rule is believed to have been marked by prosperity, justice, and peace, and his governance continues to be celebrated and emulated in India.

In addition to his cultural significance, Ram is also a beloved figure in Indian popular culture. His stories, songs, and plays are an integral part of Indian entertainment, and they continue to inspire people of all ages.

Ram is much more than just a Hindu deity. He is a symbol of values, ethics, and morality, and his story and teachings have had a profound impact on Indian society and culture.

Ram in Literature

Explore the many different literary works that feature Ram as a central character, including the Ramayana, the Mahabharata, and various other texts from across the Indian subcontinent.

Ram is a central figure in many literary works from across the Indian subcontinent, each providing a unique perspective on his character and teachings. Here are some of the most significant texts that feature Ram as a central character:

- Ramayana: This is the most well-known and revered text featuring Ram as the protagonist. The Ramayana is an epic poem composed by the sage Valmiki and tells the story of Ram's exile from his kingdom, his journey to rescue his wife Sita from the demon king Ravana, and his eventual return to his rightful place as king.
- Mahabharata: Although Ram is not the central character of the Mahabharata, he is mentioned several times throughout the epic poem. One of the most significant references to Ram in the Mahabharata is the story of his bow, which only he was able to lift and break in the

competition to win the hand of Sita.

- Puranas: The Puranas are a collection of ancient Hindu texts that tell the stories of various deities, including Ram. These texts provide more in-depth accounts of Ram's life, teachings, and the impact he had on the people of his time.
- Adhyatma Ramayana: This is a text that presents the Ramayana from a spiritual perspective, focusing on Ram's teachings and the moral lessons that can be gleaned from his story.
- Ramcharitmanas: This is a devotional text composed by the saint Tulsidas, which retells the story of Ram in a simplified form. The Ramcharitmanas is one of the most popular texts in the Hindi-speaking regions of India and is often recited in religious ceremonies.
- Krittivasi Ramayan: This is a Bengali retelling of the Ramayana, composed by the poet Krittibas Ojha in the 15th century. The Krittivasi Ramayan has a distinct regional flavour and is still widely read and revered in West Bengal.
- Ramakien: This is a Thai epic poem that retells the story of Ram in a Southeast Asian context. The Ramakien features many of the same characters as the Ramayana but adds its unique twists and turns to the narrative.

These are just a few examples of the many literary works that feature Ram as a central character. Each text provides a unique perspective on his teachings, and together they form a rich tapestry of stories and wisdom that continue to inspire people across the Indian subcontinent and beyond.

Ram in Philosophy

Philosophical underpinnings of Ram's story and explore how different schools of Hindu philosophy interpret and understand his role in the world.

The story of Ram is deeply rooted in the philosophical underpinnings of Hinduism. Ram's life and teachings are interpreted differently by different schools of Hindu philosophy, each emphasizing different aspects of his character and teachings. Here are some of the main philosophical perspectives on Ram and his role in the world

- Advaita Vedanta: This school of philosophy emphasizes the non-dual nature of reality and the ultimate unity of all beings. In this context, Ram is seen as an expression of the divine consciousness that pervades all of creation. His story serves as a metaphor for the individual soul's journey towards enlightenment and the realization of its true nature as one with the divine.
- Vishishtadvaita: This school of philosophy emphasizes the interconnectedness of all beings and the idea that the individual soul is part of a larger cosmic whole. In this context, Ram is seen as an embodiment of the divine qualities of love, compassion, and justice. His story illustrates the importance of fulfilling one's duties in life and upholding dharma, the universal law of righteousness.
- Dvaita: This school of philosophy emphasizes the dualistic nature of reality and the existence of a personal God who interacts with the world. In this context, Ram is seen as an incarnation of the God Vishnu, sent to

earth to restore order and vanquish evil. His story illustrates the importance of devotion to God and the power of divine grace in overcoming adversity.
- Yoga: This school of philosophy emphasizes the path of spiritual practice and the attainment of enlightenment through meditation and self-discipline. In this context, Ram is seen as a yogi, embodying the virtues of detachment, self-control, and compassion. His story serves as an inspiration for those seeking to follow the path of yoga and attain liberation from the cycle of birth and death.

Ram's story and teachings are interpreted differently by different schools of Hindu philosophy, each emphasizing different aspects of his character and teachings. However, all of these perspectives share a common thread of reverence and respect for Ram as a symbol of morality, ethics, and spiritual insight.

Ram in History

Delve into the historical context in which Ram's story emerged, exploring how it was influenced by the social, political, and cultural forces of its time.

The story of Ram emerged in the context of ancient India, where it was influenced by a range of social, political, and cultural forces. Here are some of the key factors that shaped the development of the Ramayana and the emergence of Ram as a cultural icon

- Vedic Religion: The Vedic religion, which preceded Hinduism, was a complex and diverse system of beliefs and practices. The earliest references to Ram can be found in the Rigveda, a collection of ancient hymns that date back to around 1500 BCE. Ram was initially portrayed as a minor deity associated with the sun and the dawn, and his story gradually evolved.
- Emergence of Hinduism: The emergence of Hinduism as a dominant religious tradition in India was a gradual process that spanned several centuries. The Ramayana, along with other epics such as the Mahabharata, played a key role in this process by providing a shared cultural narrative that helped to unify diverse communities under a common religious identity.
- Influence of Buddhism: Buddhism emerged in India during the same period as Hinduism and had a significant impact on Indian culture and philosophy. The story of Ram was influenced by Buddhist themes and motifs, such as the emphasis on compassion, non-violence, and the importance of detachment from worldly attachments.
- Political Context: The political context of ancient India was characterized by a range of kingdoms and empires that vied for power and influence. The story of Ram was often used as a political tool to legitimize the rule of monarchs and to reinforce social hierarchies based on caste and gender.
- Cultural Influences: The Ramayana drew on a wide range of cultural influences, including folk tales, legends, and myths from across India. These influences helped to shape the story of Ram and to create a rich and diverse cultural tapestry that continues to inspire generations of artists, writers, and scholars.

The story of Ram emerged in a complex and dynamic cultural context that was shaped by a range of social, political, and cultural forces. The enduring popularity of Ram and the Ramayana is a testament to their ability to capture the imagination and provide a sense of cultural identity and continuity in a rapidly changing world.

Ram in Art and Iconography:

Ram has been depicted in art, sculpture, and other forms of visual culture, and explores what these representations tell us about his place in Hindu society and culture.

Ram has been a popular subject of visual culture in India and beyond, and his depictions in art, sculpture, and other forms of visual media reflect the diversity and richness of Indian culture. Here are some of the main themes and motifs found in these representations of Ram:

- Divine Hero: Ram is often depicted as a divine hero, embodying the virtues of courage, strength, and righteousness. In these representations, he is shown carrying a bow and arrow, standing tall and proud, and radiating a sense of power and majesty.

- Devotion and Love: Another common theme in depictions of Ram is his relationship with his wife, Sita. Their love story is one of the most enduring and beloved in Indian culture, and it is often depicted in art and sculpture. These representations emphasize the deep devotion and love between the two characters, as well as the challenges and obstacles they faced in their journey together.

- Spiritual Wisdom: Ram is also revered for his spiritual wisdom and insight, and his teachings are often depicted in art and sculpture. These representations emphasize the importance of living a moral and ethical life, and they often incorporate quotes from the Ramayana and other texts.

- Iconography: Ram is associated with a range of iconographic elements that are used to identify him in art and sculpture. These include his blue skin, which represents his divine nature, as well as his bow and arrow, lotus flower, and conch shell.

- Regional Variations: The depictions of Ram in art and sculpture vary widely across different regions of India, reflecting the diversity of Indian culture. For example, in South India, Ram is often depicted with a moustache and wearing a crown, while in North India, he is typically clean-shaven and wearing a turban.

The representations of Ram in visual culture reflect the deep reverence and admiration that he inspires in Indian culture. These depictions celebrate his heroic qualities, his spiritual wisdom, and his enduring love for Sita, and they continue to inspire and captivate audiences across generations.

Ram in Popular Culture

Ram has been adapted and reinterpreted in popular culture, including in films, television shows, and other forms of media.

Ramayana is a timeless epic that has been adapted and reinterpreted in various forms of popular culture, including films, television shows, and other forms of media. Here are some of the key ways in which Ram has been portrayed in popular culture

- Film: Ram has been a popular subject in Indian cinema, and there have been numerous films made about his life and adventures. Some of the most popular include "Ram Rajya" (1943), "Ramayana: The Legend of Prince Rama" (1992), and "Ram-Leela" (2013).

- Television: The Ramayana has also been adapted into numerous television shows in India and beyond. One of the most popular versions is the "Ramayan" television series, which originally aired in the late 1980s and has since been re-broadcast many times.

- Comics and Graphic Novels: The story of Ram has also been adapted into various forms of graphic novels and comics. These adaptations often incorporate elements of modern storytelling and art styles, while remaining faithful to the original story.

- Music and Dance: The Ramayana has also been adapted into various forms of music and dance, including classical Indian dance forms like Bharatanatyam and

Kathak. These performances often incorporate elements of drama and storytelling, and they help to bring the story of Ram to life in new and exciting ways.

- Video Games: In recent years, the story of Ram has also been adapted into various video games. These games allow players to immerse themselves in the world of the Ramayana and to experience the adventures of Ram first-hand.

The adaptations and reinterpretations of Ram in popular culture reflect the enduring appeal and relevance of his story in modern times. By bringing the story of Ram to new audiences in new and innovative ways, these adaptations help to ensure that the legacy of Ram and the Ramayana will continue to inspire and captivate people for generations to come.

Ram as a Symbol of National Identity

Ram has been invoked as a symbol of national identity and unity in modern India, particularly by Hindu nationalist groups. This use of the Ram as a symbol of national identity and unity has been the subject of political and cultural debates in India, with some viewing it as a positive development and others viewing it as a dangerous form of cultural nationalism. Here are some of the key debates and controversies that have surrounded the use of Ram in this context

- Cultural Nationalism: Some critics argue that the use of the Ram as a symbol of national identity and unity is a form of cultural nationalism that seeks to promote Hindu culture and marginalize other religious and ethnic groups in India. They argue that this kind of cultural nationalism is divisive and exclusionary and that it undermines the secular and pluralistic principles of Indian democracy.

- Communal Violence: Others argue that the invocation of Ram as a symbol of national identity and unity has been linked to communal violence in India, particularly in the context of clashes between Hindus and Muslims. They argue that this kind of religious nationalism can be a source of conflict and violence and that it is, therefore, dangerous for the stability and unity of the country.

- Historical Accuracy: Some critics argue that the use of Ram as a symbol of national identity and unity is based on a distorted and ahistorical view of Indian history. They argue that the story of Ram has been used to promote a particular version of Indian history that marginalizes other cultures and religions and that this version of history is not supported by the available evidence.

- Unity and Pride: Supporters of the use of the Ram as a symbol of national identity and unity argue that it helps to promote a sense of unity and pride among Hindus in India. They argue that this kind of cultural nationalism is necessary to counter the perceived marginalization of Hindus in Indian society and that it can help to create a more cohesive and unified nation.

The use of Ram as a symbol of national identity and unity in modern India has been the subject of political and cultural debates, with critics arguing that it is a dangerous form of cultural nationalism that can lead to communal violence and undermine the secular and pluralistic principles of Indian democracy, while supporters argue that it is necessary to promote a sense of unity and pride among Hindus in India.

Ram and the Politics of Belief

The story of Ram has been used by different religious and political groups in India to advance their agendas. Here are some of the key ways in which Ram's story has been used in this context, and the tensions and conflicts that have arisen as a result:

- Hindu Nationalism: Hindu nationalist groups in India have used the story of Ram to promote a sense of Hindu identity and to assert the dominance of Hindu culture over other religions and cultures in India. This has led to tensions with religious minorities, particularly Muslims, who feel marginalized and excluded by this form of cultural nationalism.
- Dalit Assertion: Dalit activists and organizations have also used the story of Ram to advance their agenda of social and political empowerment. They have highlighted the fact that the character of Shambuka, a low-caste person who was killed by Ram, is often used to justify the oppression of Dalits in India. They have also pointed out that the Dalit saint Ravidas had a vision of Ram that challenged traditional hierarchies and power structures.

- Feminist Interpretations: Feminist scholars and activists have challenged the traditional patriarchal interpretations of Ram's story, which often portray women as passive and subservient. They have highlighted the agency and strength of female characters like Sita and Shabari, and have called for a more nuanced and complex understanding of gender roles and relationships in the Ramayana.

- Environmentalism: Environmental activists have used the story of Ram to promote ecological awareness and conservation. They have highlighted the role of forests and wildlife in the Ramayana, and have called for a more sustainable and harmonious relationship between humans and nature.

The use of Ram's story to advance different religious and political agendas has led to tensions and conflicts in Indian society. While some groups see Ram as a unifying figure who represents the best of Indian culture and tradition, others view his story as a source of division and exclusion. As India continues to grapple with these tensions, the story of Ram will likely continue to be a subject of debate and controversy in the years to come.

Ram and Contemporary Religious Practice:

Ram continues to be worshipped and venerated by millions of Hindus around the world in a variety of ways. Here are some examples of how Ram is worshipped and what his story means to people in different contexts and communities:

- Puja and Festivals: Ram is worshipped through puja, a ritualistic worship of a deity that involves offering flowers, incense, and other items, and performing specific prayers and mantras. Ram is also celebrated during festivals like Diwali, which marks his return to Ayodhya after defeating the demon king Ravana.

- Bhakti: Bhakti is the devotional worship of a deity, and many Hindus practice this form of devotion towards Ram. Bhakti involves a deep personal relationship with the deity and often includes singing hymns and songs in praise of Ram, reading and reflecting on his teachings, and striving to emulate his virtues in one's daily life.

- Social Justice: Ram's story has been used by many Hindus as a call to social justice and compassion. The character of Ram is often seen as a model of ethical leadership, and his story is used to inspire people to fight against oppression, inequality, and injustice.

- Personal Transformation: The story of Ram is also used by many Hindus as a means of personal transformation and spiritual growth. Ram's journey is seen as a metaphor for the spiritual journey of the individual, and his teachings are used to guide people towards a deeper understanding of the self and the divine.

- Cultural Identity: For many Hindus, Ram is not just a deity, but a symbol of their cultural identity and heritage. The story of Ram is seen as a source of pride and inspiration and is often used to assert the importance of Hindu culture and tradition.

In different contexts and communities, the meaning and significance of Ram's story may vary. For some, Ram is a divine figure who represents the highest ideals of Hinduism. For others, Ram is a historical figure who embodies the virtues of ethical leadership and social justice. And for still others, Ram is a cultural icon who represents the identity and heritage of the Hindu community. Regardless of how Ram is understood and worshipped, his story continues to inspire and guide millions of Hindus around the world.

summarizing the key themes and ideas covered, and reflecting on what Ram's story can teach us about religion, culture, and the human experience more broadly.

Religion is a complex and multifaceted aspect of human experience that shapes individual beliefs, social norms, and cultural practices. It can provide meaning, guidance, and community, but it can also fuel conflict, oppression, and discrimination. The study of religion involves exploring various traditions, texts, rituals, and doctrines, as well as their historical, social, and psychological dimensions.

Culture refers to the shared values, beliefs, customs, and artefacts that shape the identity and behaviour of a particular group or society. Culture can manifest in various domains such as language, art, music, cuisine, fashion, and technology. It can provide a sense of belonging and pride, but it can also create boundaries and stereotypes that limit diversity and creativity. The study of culture involves examining the diversity and complexity of human expression and interaction, as well as the power dynamics and challenges of cultural exchange.

The human experience encompasses the full range of phenomena that arise from being alive and conscious, including physical, emotional, cognitive, and spiritual dimensions. It involves navigating a complex and ever-changing world, facing various challenges and opportunities, and seeking meaning, purpose, and fulfilment. The study of the human experience involves exploring the biological, psychological, social, and cultural factors that shape human behaviour, cognition, emotion, and identity, as well as the ethical and existential questions that arise from it.

Ram's story, depending on which story is being referred to, can teach us various lessons about religion, culture, and the human experience. It can show us the diversity and complexity of human beliefs, practices, and values, as well as the power and limitations of tradition and innovation. It can also reveal the challenges and opportunities of intercultural and interfaith dialogue, as well as the importance of empathy, respect, and critical thinking in navigating the complexities of the human condition.

CHAPTER SIX

Qualities of Governance that Make Ram a Symbol of Perfection

Ram, one of the most revered deities in Hindu mythology, is often seen as a symbol of perfect governance. The story of Ram is relevant to the topic of governance because it presents a model of leadership that is just, ethical, and wise.

Here are some key themes and ideas that make Ram a symbol of perfect governance:

- Upholding the law: Ram is often depicted as a just ruler who upholds the law and punishes those who violate it. He is known for his unwavering commitment to justice, even when it comes at great personal cost. This is reflected in his decision to banish his beloved wife Sita to the forest when she is accused of infidelity, despite his deep love for her.

- Compassion and empathy: Although Ram is a strict enforcer of the law, he is also known for his compassion and empathy. He is deeply attuned to the needs and concerns of his subjects and goes to great lengths to ensure their well-being. This is exemplified in his decision to take a vow of poverty and live in exile with his wife and brother to fulfil his father's wishes.

- Trust and accountability: Ram is known for his unwavering commitment to his duties and responsibilities as a leader. He is transparent in his decision-making and accountable to his subjects, which earns him their trust and respect. This is demonstrated in his decision to consult with his advisors and seek their counsel before making important decisions.

- Courage and resilience: Ram is a fearless warrior who is not afraid to take on powerful enemies to protect his people. He is also known for his resilience in the face of adversity, as seen in his unwavering commitment to his duties despite facing numerous challenges and setbacks.

The story of Ram presents a powerful model of leadership that is just, ethical, and wise. By embodying these qualities, Ram is seen as a symbol of perfect governance and a source of inspiration for leaders across generations.

Ram's Leadership Qualities:

leadership qualities that Ram exhibited throughout his life, including his integrity, fairness, courage, and compassion, and how these qualities make him a symbol of perfect governance.

Ram, the protagonist of the Hindu epic Ramayana, is considered one of the greatest leaders in history due to his exemplary qualities of integrity, fairness, courage, and compassion. He is revered as an ideal ruler and an embodiment of perfect governance. His leadership qualities have been praised for centuries and continue to inspire leaders today. In this essay, I will discuss how Ram exhibited these qualities throughout his life and how they make him a symbol of perfect governance.

Integrity is one of the most important qualities that a leader should possess, and Ram was a prime example of this. He was known for his honesty and adherence to moral principles. Ram's integrity was evident from the beginning of the Ramayana, where he chose to obey his father's orders and leave for exile despite knowing that he was the rightful heir to the throne. He could have chosen to defy his father's orders and take the throne, but he chose to uphold his duty and his integrity.

Throughout his life, Ram was known to stand by his word and never compromise his principles. When he promised his wife Sita that he would protect her, he did everything in his power to keep his word, even when it meant fighting a war against an army much larger than his own. This unwavering commitment to his values and principles made Ram a symbol of integrity and earned him the respect and admiration of his subjects.

Fairness is another quality that Ram exemplified as a leader. He believed in treating everyone with equality and justice, regardless of their social status or background. One of the most famous incidents that illustrate Ram's fairness is when he banished his wife Sita to the forest, despite knowing that she was innocent, to uphold the public opinion of his people. Even though Sita was his beloved wife and he knew she was not guilty of any wrongdoing, he put the needs of his people above his desires.

Ram's commitment to fairness and justice extended beyond his immediate family. He was known to be fair and impartial in his dealings with his subjects, regardless of their social standing. He was always accessible to his people and would go out of his way to help them, regardless of their caste or creed. This fairness and impartiality made Ram a beloved leader who was respected and admired by all.

Courage is another quality that Ram exhibited throughout his life. He was known to be a fearless warrior who led his army from the front. He never shied away from a battle and was always ready to face any challenge that came his way. One of the most famous incidents that illustrate Ram's courage is the war with Ravana, the king of Lanka. Despite being outnumbered and outmatched, Ram led his army into battle and ultimately emerged victorious. His courage and leadership inspired his troops to fight valiantly and led to their success.

Ram's courage was not limited to the battlefield. He also

displayed courage in his personal life, such as when he chose to leave his comfortable life in the palace to live in the forest. This decision was not an easy one, as it meant giving up his rightful claim to the throne and living a life of hardship and uncertainty. However, Ram displayed tremendous courage and commitment to his values by making this decision.

Compassion is perhaps the most important quality that Ram exhibited throughout his life. He was known to be a kind and empathetic leader who cared deeply for his subjects. He was always willing to help those in need and would go out of his way to ensure their well-being. One of the most famous incidents that illustrate Ram's compassion is when he helped the poor and downtrodden, including the low-caste boatman who helped him cross the river.

Ram's compassion extended beyond his immediate circle of family and friends. He was known to be kind and empathetic towards all living beings

Ram's Approach to Justice:

Ram's approach to justice was grounded in the principles of fairness, equity, and impartiality, and how this approach can inform contemporary governance practices.

Ram's approach to justice was based on the principles of fairness, equity, and impartiality. He believed that justice should be blind, and every individual should be treated equally, regardless of social status or background. Ram's approach to justice was grounded in his understanding that every individual has inherent dignity and deserves respect and equal treatment under the law. His approach to justice has significant implications for contemporary governance practices.

One of the critical aspects of Ram's approach to justice was his commitment to fairness. He believed that justice should be impartial and that every individual should be treated fairly, regardless of their social status or background. This principle is particularly important in contemporary governance practices, where marginalized communities often face systemic discrimination and are denied access to justice. Ram's approach to justice can inform contemporary governance practices by emphasizing the need for fairness in the delivery of justice and ensuring that every individual receives equal treatment under the law.

Another critical aspect of Ram's approach to justice was his commitment to equity. He believed that justice should not only be fair, but it should also equitable. This means that every individual should receive justice that takes into account their unique circumstances and needs. Ram's approach to justice can inform contemporary governance practices by emphasizing the need for equity in the delivery of justice. This means that governance practices should consider the specific needs of marginalized communities, such as women, people of colour, and the LGBTQ+ community when delivering justice.

Ram's approach to justice was also grounded in his understanding of the importance of impartiality. He believed that justice should be blind, and every individual should be treated equally, regardless of social status or background. This principle is particularly important in contemporary governance practices, where powerful individuals often use their influence to manipulate the justice system. Ram's approach to justice can inform contemporary governance practices by emphasizing the need for impartiality in the delivery of justice. This means that governance practices should be free from bias and influence, and every individual should receive justice based on the merits of their case.

Ram's approach to justice also emphasized the importance of accountability. He believed that those in power should be held accountable for their actions and that justice should be swift and certain. Ram's approach to justice can inform contemporary governance practices by emphasizing the need for accountability in the delivery of justice. This means that those in power should be held responsible for their actions, and the justice system should be swift and certain in delivering justice.

Ram's approach to justice was grounded in the principles of fairness, equity, and impartiality. His approach to justice can inform contemporary governance practices by emphasizing the need for fairness, equity, impartiality, and accountability in the delivery of justice. Contemporary governance practices should be guided by the principles of justice, which prioritize the needs and rights of all individuals, regardless of their social status or background. By adopting Ram's approach to justice, contemporary governance practices can ensure that every individual receives justice that is fair, equitable, impartial, and accountable.

Ram's Management of Resources:

How Ram managed resources, including finances, human resources, and natural resources, and how his approach to resource management can be applied in modern governance.

Ram's approach to resource management was grounded in the principles of efficiency, effectiveness, and sustainability. He believed that resources should be used judiciously and that their utilization should be optimized to meet the needs of the people. Ram's approach to resource management has significant implications for modern governance, particularly in the areas of finance, human resources, and natural resources.

Finance Management:

Ram's approach to finance management was based on the principles of transparency and accountability. He believed that finances should be managed in a way that promotes transparency, accountability, and efficiency. Ram's approach to finance management can be applied in modern governance by emphasizing the need for transparency and accountability in financial transactions. Governance practices should ensure that all financial transactions are transparent and that the use of public funds is closely monitored to prevent corruption.

Human Resource Management:

Ram's approach to human resource management was grounded in the principles of meritocracy, fairness, and inclusiveness. He believed that human resources should be managed in a way that promotes meritocracy, fairness, and inclusiveness. Ram's approach to human resource management can be applied in modern governance by emphasizing the need for merit-based recruitment, fair treatment of employees, and inclusive policies that promote diversity and equity in the workplace.

Natural Resource Management:

Ram's approach to natural resource management was grounded in the principles of sustainability and environmental conservation. He believed that natural resources should be managed in a way that promotes sustainability and environmental conservation. Ram's approach to natural resource management can be applied in modern governance by emphasizing the need for sustainable resource utilization, conservation, and management. Governance practices should prioritize the conservation of natural resources and promote sustainable development practices that ensure the long-term availability of resources for future generations.

One of the critical aspects of Ram's approach to resource management was his emphasis on the importance of planning. He believed that resource utilization should be planned and that resources should be allocated based on the needs of the people. Ram's approach to resource management can be applied in modern governance by emphasizing the need for planning in resource management. Governance practices should ensure that resource utilization is planned and that resources are allocated based on the needs of the people.

Another critical aspect of Ram's approach to resource management was his emphasis on innovation. He believed that innovation was essential to efficient and effective resource utilization. Ram's approach to resource management can be applied in modern governance by emphasizing the need for innovation in resource management. Governance practices should encourage innovation in resource management, and explore new and innovative ways to optimize resource utilization.

Ram's approach to resource management was grounded in the principles of efficiency, effectiveness, and sustainability. His approach to resource management can be applied in modern governance by emphasizing the need for transparency and accountability in financial transactions, merit-based recruitment and fair treatment of employees, sustainable resource utilization, planning, and innovation. By adopting Ram's approach to resource management, modern governance practices can optimize resource utilization, promote sustainability, and ensure the long-term availability of resources for future generations

Ram's Relationship with Citizens:

How Ram maintained a strong and positive relationship with the citizens he governed, including how he listened to their needs, engaged them in decision-making, and maintained transparency and accountability.

Ram maintained a strong and positive relationship with the citizens he governed by prioritizing their needs and engaging them in decision-making processes. He believed in the importance of listening to the people he governed and addressing their concerns, which helped to build trust and respect between himself and his subjects. Ram's approach to governance can provide valuable lessons for modern governance practices.

Listening to the Needs of Citizens

Ram was known for his ability to listen to the needs of his citizens. He regularly engaged with the people he governed and addressed their concerns. Ram's approach to governance can be applied in modern governance by emphasizing the importance of listening to citizens and addressing their needs. Governance practices should ensure that citizens' voices are heard and that they are included in decision-making processes.

Engaging Citizens in Decision-Making:

Ram believed in the importance of engaging citizens in decision-making processes. He consulted with his advisors and sought the opinions of his citizens before making important decisions. Ram's approach to governance can be applied in modern governance by emphasizing the importance of citizen engagement in decision-making processes. Governance practices should ensure that citizens are included in decision-making processes and that their opinions are valued.

Transparency and Accountability:

Ram was known for his transparency and accountability in governance. He kept detailed records of his administration, including financial transactions and other important decisions. Ram's approach to governance can be applied in modern governance by emphasizing the importance of transparency and accountability. Governance practices should ensure that information is readily available to the public and that there are mechanisms in place to hold officials accountable for their actions.

In modern governance, some challenges may hinder the ability to maintain strong and positive relationships with citizens. These challenges include rapid urbanization, increasing economic disparities, and political polarization. Governance practices can learn from Ram's approach to governance to address these challenges.

Rapid Urbanization

Ram governed during a time when most people lived in rural areas. Today, however, rapid urbanization has led to the growth of cities and towns, which can make it challenging to maintain strong relationships with citizens. Governance practices can address this challenge by using technology to engage with citizens, providing regular updates on government activities through social media and other online platforms, and establishing neighbourhood associations to facilitate communication and collaboration.

Increasing Economic Disparities

Ram governed during a time when there were relatively few economic disparities between citizens. Today, however, income and wealth disparities are growing, which can create social and political tensions. Governance practices can address this challenge by implementing policies that promote economic equality, such as progressive taxation, social welfare programs, and investments in education and job training.

Political Polarization

Ram governed during a time when there was relative political stability in his kingdom. Today, however, political polarization has led to increasing divisions between citizens, making it challenging to maintain positive relationships with all citizens. Governance practices can address this challenge by promoting civic education, encouraging civil discourse, and establishing mechanisms for conflict resolution.

Ram maintained a strong and positive relationship with the citizens he governed by prioritizing their needs, engaging them in decision-making processes, and maintaining transparency and accountability. His approach to governance provides valuable lessons for modern governance practices, particularly in areas such as listening to the needs of citizens, engaging citizens in decision-making, and promoting transparency and accountability. By learning from Ram's approach to governance, modern governance practices can address challenges such as rapid urbanization, increasing economic disparities, and political polarization, build strong and positive relationships with citizens.

Ram's Role in Establishing Good Governance:

Ram's reign is characterized by good governance practices that have continued to inspire people across the world. Here are some of the practices that characterized Ram's rule and how they compare with contemporary governance:

- Rule of Law: Ram was a strong believer in the rule of law. He ensured that the law applied equally to all citizens, regardless of their status or caste. This was evident in his decision to banish his wife, Sita, when doubts were raised about her fidelity. Ram's commitment to the rule of law continues to be an important principle in contemporary governance around the world.
- Accountability: Ram believed that he was accountable to his people for his actions. He was willing to listen to the concerns of his subjects and take action to address them. This accountability ensured that he remained popular among his people and was able to maintain peace and order in his kingdom.
- Participation: Ram believed in the importance of participation and inclusivity in governance. He encouraged the participation of all citizens in the decision-making process, and his administration was known for being accessible to all. This practice has continued to inform contemporary governance practices, with many governments now promoting citizen participation in decision-making processes.

In contemporary governance, there are similarities and differences with the governance practices during Ram's reign. For example, many governments around the world today continue to promote the principles of the rule of law, accountability, and participation. However, there are also instances where these principles are violated, such as in cases of corruption or authoritarian regimes.

Furthermore, contemporary governance practices have also evolved to address new challenges, such as globalization and the need to address climate change. As such, there are now new governance practices such as international cooperation, sustainable development goals, and digital governance that are becoming increasingly important.

Ram's legacy of good governance practices has continued to inspire people around the world, and his principles of rule of law, accountability, and participation remain relevant today. However, contemporary governance has also evolved to address new challenges, and new practices have emerged to promote more effective governance in the 21st century.

Ram's Influence on Indian Political Thought:

How Ram's story has influenced Indian political thought and governance practices, including the role he plays in contemporary debates over secularism, diversity, and democracy.

Ram's story has been interpreted and adapted in many ways over the centuries. Here are some of how Ram's story has influenced Indian political thought and governance practices:

- Hindu Nationalism: In contemporary Indian politics, Ram has become a symbol of Hindu nationalism. Hindu nationalists believe that India is a Hindu nation, and they seek to promote Hindu culture and values in Indian society. The construction of a Ram temple in Ayodhya has been a long-standing demand of Hindu nationalists, who believe that it will help to promote Hindu identity and unity.
- Secularism: Ram's story has also been interpreted in more secular ways, with some seeing him as a symbol of good governance and ethical leadership. The idea of Ram Rajya, or the rule of Ram, has been used to promote a vision of a just and equitable society, where the principles of the rule of law and accountability are upheld. This vision of Ram Rajya is often seen as a more inclusive and secular interpretation of Ram's story, which emphasizes his ethical leadership and good governance practices.
- Diversity: Another important aspect of Ram's story is its emphasis on diversity and pluralism. Ram is often portrayed as a king who was just and fair to all his subjects, regardless of their caste or social status. This emphasis on diversity and pluralism has been an important influence on contemporary debates over democracy and inclusion in Indian society.
- Democracy: Ram's story has also influenced Indian political thought and governance practices in its emphasis on democracy and the importance of public

participation. Ram's reign is often seen as an example of how a just and equitable society can be achieved through democratic governance and citizen participation.

In contemporary debates over secularism, diversity, and democracy, Ram's story continues to play an important role. His story is often used to promote different visions of Indian society, ranging from Hindu nationalism to more inclusive and secular interpretations of his legacy. Ultimately, the impact of Ram's story on Indian political thought and governance practices is a complex and ongoing process, shaped by a wide range of social, political, and cultural factors.

Ram in Comparative Perspective:

How Ram's approach to governance compares to other historical and contemporary leaders and governance models from around the world, highlighting the similarities and differences between them.

Ram's approach to governance was characterized by a strong commitment to the rule of law, accountability, and participation. There are many other historical and contemporary leaders and governance models from around the world that share these values, but there are also significant differences between them. Here are some examples of how Ram's approach to governance compares to other historical and contemporary leaders and governance models:

- Mahatma Gandhi: Gandhi was a key figure in India's struggle for independence and a proponent of nonviolent resistance. Like Ram, Gandhi believed in the importance of ethical leadership and good governance practices, such as accountability and citizen participation. However, Gandhi also emphasized the importance of spiritual and moral values in governance, such as the principle of ahimsa (nonviolence).
- Nelson Mandela: Mandela was a key figure in the fight against apartheid in South Africa and a champion of democracy and human rights. Like Ram, Mandela believed in the importance of accountability and citizen participation in governance, but he also emphasized the importance of reconciliation and forgiveness as key values in building a just and equitable society.
- Scandinavian countries: Scandinavian countries, such as Norway, Sweden, and Denmark, are often cited as examples of successful social democracies. These countries have high levels of social welfare and strong public services, and they place a strong emphasis on equality and social justice. Like Ram, the Scandinavian countries prioritize the rule of law and citizen participation, but they also place a strong emphasis on collective responsibility and social welfare.
- Singapore: Singapore is often cited as an example of successful authoritarianism, with a strong focus on economic growth and efficiency. Like Ram, Singapore places a strong emphasis on good governance practices, such as the rule of law and accountability, but it also places a strong emphasis on centralized control and economic development, often at the expense of individual freedoms and civil liberties.

In comparing these different leaders and governance models to Ram's approach to governance, it becomes clear that there are similarities and differences between them. While they may share some values, such as the importance of the rule of law and citizen participation, they also differ in their emphasis on other values, such as spirituality, social welfare, or economic development. Ultimately, the success of a governance model depends on a wide range of factors, including social, economic, and cultural contexts, as well as the individual values and leadership styles of the leaders involved.

Criticisms and Controversies:

Explore criticisms and controversies surrounding Ram's legacy, including debates over his treatment of women and marginalized groups, and how these critiques can inform ongoing efforts to improve governance practices.

While Ram is often celebrated for his good governance practices, there are also criticisms and controversies surrounding his legacy, particularly about his treatment of women and marginalized groups. These critiques can inform ongoing efforts to improve governance practices in India.

Treatment of Women: One of the most common criticisms of Ram's legacy is his treatment of women, particularly his treatment of his wife, Sita. In the Ramayana, Sita is often portrayed as a submissive and obedient wife who is expected to follow her husband's every command, even when he banishes her from the kingdom. This portrayal has been criticized as patriarchal and misogynistic and has been used to justify violence against women in India.

Treatment of Dalits: Another criticism of Ram's legacy is his treatment of Dalits, who were traditionally considered to be part of the lowest caste in Indian society. While Ram is often portrayed as a just and fair ruler, his treatment of Dalits has been criticized as discriminatory and oppressive. In some versions of the Ramayana, Dalits are portrayed as unclean and unworthy of respect, which has contributed to their marginalization and oppression in Indian society.

These critiques can inform ongoing efforts to improve governance practices in India by highlighting the importance of addressing issues of gender and caste-based discrimination in governance. Efforts to promote gender equality and social justice in governance can help to promote a more inclusive and equitable society, where the rights and dignity of all citizens are respected. Additionally, efforts to promote transparency, accountability, and citizen participation can help to promote good governance practices, where the needs and interests of all citizens are represented and protected. By addressing these criticisms and controversies, Indian governance can strive towards a more just and equitable society.

The story of Ram is rich in themes and ideas that can teach us valuable lessons about governance, leadership, and the human experience. Some of the key themes and ideas include:

The importance of ethical leadership: Ram is often portrayed as a just and fair ruler, who prioritizes the well-being of his subjects over his interests. His commitment to ethical leadership, which includes principles such as accountability, transparency, and the rule of law, can serve as a model for contemporary leaders and governance practices.

The role of diversity and inclusion in governance: The story of Ram highlights the importance of diversity and inclusion in governance, particularly in terms of caste and gender. Ram's treatment of marginalized groups, such as Dalits and women, can serve as a reminder of the need for governance practices that promote social justice and equality.

The power of human relationships: The story of Ram is also a powerful reminder of the importance of human relationships in governance and leadership. Ram's relationship with his wife, Sita, and his brother, Laxman, highlights the importance of trust, loyalty, and mutual support in leadership and governance.

The challenges of leadership and decision-making: The story of Ram also highlights the challenges of leadership and decision-making, particularly in times of crisis. Ram's decision to banish Sita from the kingdom, for example, was difficult and controversial, but it ultimately reflects his commitment to upholding the rule of law and protecting the interests of his subjects.

In reflecting on what Ram's story can teach us about governance, leadership, and the human experience more broadly, it becomes clear that these themes and ideas are timeless and universal. They apply not just to governance and leadership, but to all areas of human life. The story of Ram reminds us of the importance of ethical principles, diversity and inclusion, human relationships, and the challenges of decision-making and leadership. By reflecting on these themes and ideas, we can strive towards a more just and equitable society, where the rights and dignity of all citizens are respected and protected.

CHAPTER SEVEN

Relevance of Ram Rajya in Promoting a Sustainable and inclusive world

Ram Rajya refers to the ideal kingdom or reign of Lord Rama, one of the most revered deities in Hinduism. According to Hindu mythology, Lord Rama was an incarnation of Lord Vishnu and is considered to be the embodiment of righteousness, morality, and compassion.

Ram Rajya is seen as a utopian society in which people lived in harmony, peace, and prosperity. The concept of Ram Rajya emphasizes the importance of virtues such as justice, truthfulness, compassion, and righteousness. In Ram Rajya, everyone was equal, and there was no discrimination based on caste, gender, or religion.

The idea of Ram Rajya is significant in Hinduism as it represents the ultimate goal of human existence - to achieve peace, harmony, and prosperity in society. The concept of Ram Rajya also highlights the importance of the ideal ruler who governs with wisdom, fairness, and compassion. Lord Rama is seen as the perfect king who ruled with these virtues, and his life serves as a role model for individuals to follow.

Some of the key themes and ideas of Ram Rajya include:

Justice: In Ram Rajya, justice was dispensed fairly and without bias. The ruler was responsible for ensuring that all individuals received justice, regardless of their social status or background.

Equality: Ram Rajya was a society where everyone was equal. There was no discrimination based on caste, gender, or religion.

Compassion: The ruler of Ram Rajya was expected to rule with compassion and empathy. He was responsible for the welfare of all his subjects, and his actions were guided by a sense of empathy and concern for their well-being.

Truthfulness: Honesty and truthfulness were highly valued in Ram Rajya. The ruler was expected to be honest and transparent in his dealings, and his subjects were expected to follow his example.

Dharma: Ram Rajya was a society where dharma or righteousness was highly valued. Individuals were expected to follow their dharma and lead a life of virtue and morality.

Ram Rajya represents the ideal society where people lived in harmony and peace. The concept of Ram Rajya emphasizes the importance of virtues such as justice, equality, compassion, truthfulness, and dharma. It serves as a model for individuals to follow and aspire to in their own lives.

Ram Rajya and Universal Values

How the principles of Ram Rajya, such as justice, fairness, compassion, and righteousness, are universal values that are relevant to all religions and faiths.

The principles of Ram Rajya, such as justice, fairness, compassion, and righteousness, are universal values that are relevant to all religions and faiths. These values are not limited to Hinduism but are shared by many other religions and faiths around the world. Here are some examples of how these principles are relevant to other religions and faiths

Justice: The principle of justice is found in all religions and faiths. It is an essential value that promotes fairness, equality, and impartiality. The Quran, the holy book of Islam, states, "O you who believe, be steadfast in the cause of Allah, bearing witness in justice. And let not the hatred of a people prevent you from being just. Be just; that is nearer to righteousness" (Surah Al-Maidah 5:8). This verse highlights the importance of justice in Islam and encourages Muslims to be fair and impartial in their dealings with others.

Fairness: The principle of fairness is also a universal value that is shared by many religions and faiths. In Christianity, the concept of fairness is closely related to the idea of love.

Jesus Christ taught his followers to love their neighbours as themselves and to treat others with fairness and kindness. The Bible states, "Do unto others as you would have them do unto you" (Luke 6:31), which emphasizes the importance of treating others with fairness and respect.

Compassion: Compassion is another universal value that is found in all religions and faiths. In Buddhism, the principle of compassion is central to the teachings of Buddha. The Buddha taught his followers to have compassion for all living beings and to alleviate the suffering of others. Similarly, in Hinduism, the principle of compassion is emphasized through the concept of seva, which means selfless service to others.

Righteousness: The principle of righteousness is also a universal value that is shared by many religions and faiths. In Judaism, the concept of righteousness is closely related to the idea of justice. The Torah, the holy book of Judaism, states, "Justice, justice shall you pursue" (Deuteronomy 16:20), which emphasizes the importance of righteousness and justice in Jewish teachings.

The principles of Ram Rajya, such as justice, fairness, compassion, and righteousness, are universal values that are relevant to all religions and faiths. These values promote peace, harmony, and prosperity in society and are essential for building a just and equitable world.

Ram Rajya and Ethics

How Ram Rajya embodies ethical principles that are shared across different religions and faiths, and how these principles can inform contemporary ethical debates and challenges.

Ram Rajya embodies ethical principles that are shared across different religions and faiths, such as justice, fairness, compassion, and righteousness. These ethical principles can inform contemporary ethical debates and challenges in various ways. Here are some examples:

Justice: The principle of justice is essential in contemporary ethical debates, particularly in discussions of social justice and human rights. The idea of justice in Ram Rajya emphasizes fairness, impartiality, and equality. These principles can inform contemporary debates on issues such as income inequality, racial and gender discrimination, and environmental justice.

Fairness: The principle of fairness is also relevant in contemporary ethical debates. In today's society, issues such as fair trade, fair access to resources, and fair distribution of wealth are often debated. The idea of fairness in Ram Rajya can inform these debates by emphasizing the importance of equitable distribution of resources and opportunities.

Compassion: Compassion is another ethical principle that can inform contemporary ethical debates. In today's world, issues such as refugee crises, poverty, and inequality often require compassion and empathy. The idea of compassion in Ram Rajya emphasizes the importance of caring for others and alleviating their suffering.

Righteousness: The principle of righteousness is relevant in contemporary ethical debates on issues such as corruption, corporate social responsibility, and ethical leadership. The idea of righteousness in Ram Rajya emphasizes the importance of moral and ethical behaviour in all aspects of life, including politics, business, and personal life.

The ethical principles embodied in Ram Rajya can inform contemporary ethical debates and challenges in various ways. These principles can provide guidance and inspiration for building a just and equitable society that promotes fairness, compassion, and righteousness. By drawing upon these ethical principles, individuals and societies can work towards creating a world that is more peaceful, harmonious, and prosperous for all.

Ram Rajya and Governance:

How the principles of Ram Rajya, such as the rule of law, accountability, and participation, can inform good governance practices that are relevant to all religions and faiths.

The principles of Ram Rajya, such as the rule of law, accountability, and participation, can inform good governance practices that are relevant to all religions and faiths. Here are some ways in which these principles can inform good governance practices:

Rule of law: The principle of the rule of law is central

to good governance practices. It promotes fairness, transparency, and accountability in government decision-making. In Ram Rajya, the rule of law was upheld by the king who acted as the guardian of the law and ensured that justice was served. This principle can inform good governance practices by emphasizing the importance of a legal system that is fair, impartial, and accessible to all.

Accountability: The principle of accountability is also essential in good governance practices. It promotes transparency, responsibility, and answerability in government decision-making. In Ram Rajya, the king was accountable to his people and had to justify his decisions to them. This principle can inform good governance practices by emphasizing the importance of holding government officials accountable for their actions and ensuring that they act in the best interest of the public.

Participation: The principle of participation is crucial in good governance practices. It promotes inclusivity, democracy, and public engagement in government decision-making. In Ram Rajya, the king consulted with his people and sought their input in decision-making. This principle can inform good governance practices by emphasizing the importance of engaging with the public, listening to their concerns, and involving them in the decision-making process.

By applying these principles to contemporary governance practices, governments can promote transparency, accountability, and public participation. These principles can also help to address some of the challenges that governments face, such as corruption, lack of trust, and poor service delivery. Moreover, these principles are universal and can be applied to all religions and faiths, irrespective of cultural and religious differences.

The principles of Ram Rajya, such as the rule of law, accountability, and participation, can inform good governance practices that are relevant to all religions and faiths. By applying these principles, governments can promote transparency, accountability, and public participation, which are essential for building a just and equitable society.

Ram Rajya and Social Justice

How Ram Rajya prioritized social justice and equity, and how these principles can be applied to address contemporary social and economic inequalities.

Ram Rajya prioritized social justice and equity by promoting a society that was based on fairness, equality, and compassion. These principles can be applied to address contemporary social and economic inequalities in various ways. Here are some examples:

Fair distribution of resources: In Ram Rajya, the king was responsible for ensuring that resources were distributed fairly among all members of society. This principle can be applied to contemporary societies by promoting fair distribution of resources such as land, water, and natural resources. Governments can also promote fair taxation policies that ensure that the burden of taxation is distributed equitably.

Equality of opportunity: Ram Rajya emphasized the importance of equality of opportunity. This principle can be applied to contemporary societies by promoting equal access to education, healthcare, and employment opportunities. Governments can also implement affirmative action policies that promote the social and economic inclusion of marginalized communities.

Compassion towards the disadvantaged: In Ram Rajya, the king was responsible for ensuring that the needs of the disadvantaged were met. This principle can be applied to contemporary societies by promoting compassion towards disadvantaged communities such as refugees, the homeless, and those living in poverty. Governments can implement social welfare policies that provide support to those who are in need.

Justice for all: Ram Rajya promoted justice for all members of society. This principle can be applied to contemporary societies by promoting the rule of law and ensuring that all individuals are treated equally before the law. Governments can also implement policies that address discrimination based on gender, race, religion, or other social identities.

The principles of social justice and equity that were prioritized in Ram Rajya can be applied to address contemporary social and economic inequalities. By promoting fair distribution of resources, equality of opportunity, compassion towards the disadvantaged, and justice for all, governments can work towards building a just and equitable society. These principles are universal and can be applied in all religions and faiths, irrespective of cultural and religious differences.

Ram Rajya and Environment

How Ram Rajya was characterized by a deep respect for the environment and the natural world, and how this perspective can inform contemporary environmental ethics and practices.

Ram Rajya was characterized by a deep respect for the environment and the natural world. This perspective can inform contemporary environmental ethics and practices in several ways. Here are some examples:

Respect for nature: In Ram Rajya, nature was considered sacred, and its preservation was a priority. This perspective can inform contemporary environmental ethics by emphasizing the importance of respecting nature and recognizing its intrinsic value.

Sustainable use of natural resources: In Ram Rajya, the king was responsible for ensuring that natural resources were used sustainably. This perspective can inform contemporary environmental practices by promoting sustainable use of natural resources such as water, land, and forests.

Conservation of biodiversity: Ram Rajya emphasized the importance of conserving biodiversity. This perspective can inform contemporary environmental practices by promoting the conservation of endangered species and their habitats.

Responsible waste management: In Ram Rajya, waste was managed responsibly, and pollution was minimized. This perspective can inform contemporary environmental practices by promoting responsible waste management and reducing pollution.

By applying these principles to contemporary environmental ethics and practices, individuals and governments can promote sustainable development and protect the environment. These principles can also help to address some of the environmental challenges that the world faces, such as climate change, deforestation, and loss of biodiversity.

The perspective of deep respect for the environment and the natural world that characterized Ram Rajya can inform contemporary environmental ethics and practices. By promoting respect for nature, sustainable use of natural resources, conservation of biodiversity, and responsible waste management, individuals and governments can work towards building a sustainable future for all. These principles are universal and can be applied in all religions and faiths, irrespective of cultural and religious differences.

Ram Rajya and Interfaith Relations

How the principles of Ram Rajya can foster interfaith dialogue, understanding, and cooperation, and how they can contribute to building a more peaceful and harmonious world.

The principles of Ram Rajya, with their emphasis on justice, fairness, compassion, and respect, can foster interfaith dialogue, understanding, and cooperation. By promoting these principles, individuals and communities can work towards building a more peaceful and harmonious world. Here are some ways in which the principles of Ram Rajya can contribute to interfaith dialogue and cooperation:

Shared values: The principles of Ram Rajya emphasize values such as justice, fairness, compassion, and respect, which are shared by many religions and faiths. By highlighting these shared values, individuals and communities can find common ground for interfaith dialogue and cooperation.

Respect for diversity: In Ram Rajya, diversity was respected and celebrated. This perspective can inform contemporary interfaith dialogue by promoting respect for the diversity of beliefs, cultures, and traditions.

Mutual understanding: The principles of Ram Rajya emphasize the importance of mutual understanding and respect. This perspective can inform contemporary interfaith dialogue by promoting active listening, open-mindedness, and empathy.

Collaboration for the common good: In Ram Rajya, collaboration for the common good was a priority. This perspective can inform contemporary interfaith cooperation by promoting joint action on issues such as poverty, social injustice, and environmental degradation.

By promoting these principles, individuals and communities can work towards building a more peaceful and harmonious world. These principles can help to overcome religious and cultural differences and promote mutual respect and understanding. They can also help to address some of the global challenges that the world faces, such as poverty, inequality, and environmental degradation. In conclusion, the principles of Ram Rajya can contribute to fostering interfaith dialogue, understanding, and cooperation, and building a more peaceful and harmonious world.

Ram Rajya and Nonviolence

How Ram Rajya is rooted in the principle of nonviolence, and how this principle can inform contemporary efforts to promote peace and conflict resolution.

Ram Rajya is rooted in the principle of nonviolence, which is also known as ahimsa. This principle can inform contemporary efforts to promote peace and conflict resolution in several ways:

Nonviolent communication: In Ram Rajya, nonviolent communication was valued, and conflicts were resolved through peaceful means. This perspective can inform contemporary conflict resolution efforts by promoting nonviolent communication, active listening, and empathy.

Conflict transformation: In Ram Rajya, conflicts were transformed into opportunities for growth and learning. This perspective can inform contemporary conflict resolution efforts by promoting conflict transformation, which involves turning conflicts into opportunities for mutual understanding and growth.

Peaceful coexistence: In Ram Rajya, peaceful coexistence was a priority, and all individuals were treated with respect and dignity. This perspective can inform contemporary efforts to promote peace by emphasizing the importance of peaceful coexistence and respect for diversity.

Forgiveness and reconciliation: In Ram Rajya, forgiveness and reconciliation were important values. This perspective can inform contemporary efforts to promote peace by emphasizing the importance of forgiveness and reconciliation as means of healing and restoring relationships.

By promoting the principle of nonviolence, individuals and communities can work towards building a more peaceful and harmonious world. This principle can help to overcome conflicts, promote mutual understanding and respect, and build relationships based on trust and cooperation. It can also help to address some of the global challenges that the world faces, such as terrorism, war, and violence.

The principle of nonviolence that is rooted in Ram Rajya can inform contemporary efforts to promote peace and conflict resolution. By promoting nonviolent communication, conflict transformation, peaceful coexistence, forgiveness, and reconciliation, individuals and communities can work towards building a more peaceful and harmonious world.

Criticisms and Controversies

criticisms and controversies surrounding the idea of Ram Rajya, including critiques of its historical and cultural context, and how these critiques can inform ongoing efforts to apply its principles in contemporary contexts.

The idea of Ram Rajya has been subject to various criticisms and controversies, particularly about its historical and cultural context. Some of the main critiques are:

Historical accuracy: One of the main criticisms of the idea of Ram Rajya is that it is based on mythological narratives rather than historical facts. Some scholars argue that the idea of Ram Rajya is a product of a particular cultural and historical context, and cannot be applied to contemporary contexts without taking into account the historical and cultural context in which it emerged.

Caste system: Another criticism of the idea of Ram Rajya is that it reinforces the caste system, which is a deeply entrenched social hierarchy in Hinduism. Some critics argue that the idea of Ram Rajya is based on a hierarchical social order, in which the king is the ultimate authority and the rest of society is subservient to him.

Gender roles: The idea of Ram Rajya has also been criticized for its gender roles. Some critics argue that the ideal of Sita, who is the epitome of female virtue in Ram Rajya, reinforces patriarchal gender norms and reinforces the idea of women as submissive and obedient.

Religious exclusivism: Some critics argue that the idea of Ram Rajya is exclusive to Hinduism and cannot be applied to other religions or faiths. This perspective can be seen as promoting religious exclusivism and ignoring the diversity of religious and cultural traditions.

These criticisms and controversies can inform ongoing efforts to apply the principles of Ram Rajya in contemporary contexts. For example, to apply the principles of Ram Rajya in a contemporary context, it is important to consider the historical and cultural context in which it emerged and to avoid reinforcing social hierarchies and promoting exclusivism. Additionally, it is important to recognize and challenge patriarchal gender norms and promote gender equality.

while the principles of Ram Rajya have much to offer in terms of ethical and governance practices, it is important to acknowledge and address the criticisms and controversies surrounding its historical and cultural context. By doing so, we can apply its principles in a more nuanced and inclusive way that is relevant to contemporary contexts.

Conclusion:
summarizing the key themes and ideas covered, and reflecting on how Ram Rajya can serve as a source of inspiration and guidance for people of all religions and faiths who are committed to building a more just, peaceful, and sustainable world.

Ram Rajya is a concept in Hinduism that describes an ideal society ruled by justice, compassion, righteousness, and fairness. It embodies several key themes and ideas that are relevant to people of all religions and faiths who are committed to building a more just, peaceful, and sustainable world. These include:

Rule of law: Ram Rajya emphasizes the importance of the rule of law, which means that everyone, including the rulers, is subject to the law. This principle is essential for creating a just and fair society, where everyone is equal before the law.

Accountability: In Ram Rajya, rulers are accountable to the people they govern. They must act in the best interest of the people and be transparent in their actions. This principle promotes good governance and helps to prevent corruption and abuse of power.

Participation: Ram Rajya emphasizes the importance of the participation of all members of society in decision-making processes. This principle promotes democracy and helps to ensure that the voices of all people are heard and their needs and concerns are addressed.

Social justice: Ram Rajya prioritizes social justice and equity. It emphasizes the importance of treating all members of society equally, regardless of their caste, class, or gender. This principle promotes a more just and equitable society, where everyone has access to necessities and opportunities.

Environmentalism: Ram Rajya is characterized by a deep respect for the environment and the natural world. This principle promotes sustainability and encourages people to live in harmony with nature.

Nonviolence: Ram Rajya is rooted in the principle of nonviolence. This principle emphasizes the importance of resolving conflicts through peaceful means and promoting compassion and understanding.

Ram Rajya can serve as a source of inspiration and guidance for people of all religions and faiths who are committed to building a more just, peaceful, and sustainable world. By embracing the principles of Ram Rajya, individuals and communities can work towards creating a society that is fair, accountable, participatory, socially just, environmentally responsible, and nonviolent.

Ram Rajya's principles can be applied in various contexts, including governance, social justice, environmentalism, and conflict resolution. For example, in governance, the principles of the rule of law, accountability, and participation can inform good governance practices that are relevant to all religions and faiths. In social justice, the principles of social justice and equity can be applied to address contemporary social and economic inequalities. In environmentalism, the principles of environmentalism can be applied to promote sustainability and protect the natural world. And in conflict resolution, the principle of nonviolence can be applied to promote peace and harmony.

Ram Rajya is a concept that embodies several key themes and ideas that are relevant to people of all religions and faiths who are committed to building a more just, peaceful, and sustainable world. Its principles can serve as a source of inspiration and guidance for individuals and communities in various contexts. By embracing these principles, we can create a better future for ourselves and future generations.

CHAPTER EIGHT

Ram Mandir embodies the principles of ideal governance

The Ram Mandir, also known as the Ram Janmabhoomi Temple, is a Hindu temple located in the city of Ayodhya in the northern Indian state of Uttar Pradesh. The temple is dedicated to Lord Ram, one of the most revered Hindu deities, and is considered one of the holiest sites in Hinduism.

Historically, the Ram Mandir is believed to have been built in the 10th century AD by the King of Ayodhya, Raja Paramadi, on the site where Lord Ram is believed to have been born. The temple was destroyed and rebuilt several times over the centuries, with the most recent demolition occurring in 1992 by Hindu activists who claimed that the original temple had been destroyed by Muslim rulers and replaced with a mosque, the Babri Masjid.

The Ram Mandir has been a symbol of Hindu-Muslim tensions in India for decades, with both communities claiming ownership of the site. However, in 2019, the Supreme Court of India ruled in favour of building a Ram Mandir on the disputed site and ordered the construction of a new temple.

Culturally, the Ram Mandir is an important symbol of Hindu identity and pride, as Lord Ram is considered the embodiment of righteousness, morality, and duty. The temple also serves as a pilgrimage site for millions of Hindus from all over India and the world who come to seek the blessings of Lord Ram.

In terms of governance, the Ram Mandir embodies the principles of ideal governance in several ways. Firstly, the construction of the temple was carried out through a legal and constitutional process, demonstrating respect for the rule of law and due process. Secondly, the temple represents a coming together of different communities and a resolution of a long-standing dispute, showcasing the importance of dialogue, compromise, and peaceful coexistence in governance. Finally, the temple is being constructed through donations from millions of ordinary citizens, showcasing the power of public participation and voluntary contribution to governance.

Ram Mandir and Symbolism:

Explore the symbolism of the Ram Mandir, including how its architecture, design, and religious practices reflect the principles of ideal governance.

The Ram Mandir is not only a religious site for Hindus, but it is also a symbol of cultural, social, and political significance in India. The architecture, design, and religious practices of the temple reflect the principles of ideal governance in several ways.

Architecture and Design:

The architecture of the Ram Mandir is a blend of North Indian temple architecture and contemporary design. The temple's design incorporates elements of the ancient Vastu Shastra principles of Hindu architecture, which emphasize the harmony between nature, human beings, and the divine. The temple's construction is based on the Shilp Shastra, an ancient Indian treatise on architecture and sculpture, which sets the standards for the design, dimensions, and construction of temples.

The temple's structure is built using traditional materials such as sandstone and marble, reflecting the importance of preserving cultural heritage and traditional craftsmanship. The temple's central dome is designed to resemble the crown of Lord Ram, with 12 pillars representing the 12 Jyotirlingas, which are the most sacred Hindu shrines dedicated to Lord Shiva. The temple's outer walls are adorned with intricate carvings depicting scenes from the Ramayana, the Hindu epic that tells the story of Lord Ram's life and deeds.

Religious Practices:

The Ram Mandir follows the traditional Hindu religious practices of worship, including daily puja (worship), aarti (ritual offering of light), and the recitation of sacred hymns and chants. The temple is managed by the Ram Janmabhoomi Teerth Kshetra Trust, which is responsible for overseeing the temple's operations, maintenance, and development.

The temple's religious practices reflect the principles of ideal governance by promoting inclusiveness, tolerance, and respect for diversity. The temple welcomes people of all castes, religions, and backgrounds to visit and worship at the temple. The temple's management has also expressed its commitment to promoting interfaith harmony and peace.

The symbolism of the Ram Mandir extends beyond its architecture, design, and religious practices. The temple represents the power of public participation and voluntary contribution to governance. The temple's construction is being financed through donations from millions of ordinary citizens, demonstrating the importance of public participation and collective action in achieving shared goals.

The Ram Mandir is not only a religious site but also a symbol of India's rich cultural heritage, social cohesion, and political stability. The temple's architecture, design, and religious practices embody the principles of ideal governance by promoting inclusiveness, tolerance, and respect for diversity, and showcasing the power of public participation and collective action in governance.

Ram Mandir and Social Justice:

How the Ram Mandir can serve as a symbol of social justice and equity, including its role in promoting religious tolerance and unity.

The construction of the temple on the site of a former mosque has been a long-standing issue of religious conflict in India, with the dispute over the site's ownership between Hindus and Muslims going back several decades. However, the resolution of this dispute through legal means and peaceful negotiations is a symbol of social justice and equity, as it represents a coming together of different communities and a recognition of their respective rights.

The Ram Mandir can also serve as a symbol of social justice and equity by promoting religious tolerance and unity. Lord Ram is revered by millions of Hindus as the embodiment of righteousness, morality, and duty, and his story and teachings are an inspiration to people of all faiths. The temple can serve as a platform for promoting the values of compassion, empathy, and mutual respect, which are essential for building a just and equitable society.

The construction of the Ram Mandir has raised concerns about the potential for religious tensions and communal violence. However, the temple's management has expressed its commitment to promoting interfaith harmony and peace, and the construction process has been carried out with the participation of people from all communities. This inclusiveness and respect for diversity are essential elements of social justice and equity.

Furthermore, the Ram Mandir can serve as a symbol of social justice and equity by promoting public participation and collective action. The construction of the temple is being financed through donations from millions of ordinary citizens, reflecting the power of public participation and collective action in achieving shared goals. This participation and contribution can also serve as a symbol of social justice and equity by giving voice and agency to ordinary people and promoting their empowerment.

Ram Mandir can serve as a symbol of social justice and equity by promoting religious tolerance and unity, recognizing the rights of different communities, and encouraging public participation and collective action. As India moves forward on its path towards social justice and equity, the Ram Mandir can play a vital role in building a more inclusive and harmonious society.

Ram Mandir and Environmental Sustainability:

How the Ram Mandir embodies the principles of environmental sustainability, including its use of renewable resources and traditional building methods.

The Ram Mandir, located in Ayodhya, India, embodies the principles of environmental sustainability through its use of renewable resources and traditional building methods.

One of the significant aspects of the temple's construction is the use of traditional building techniques that are environment-friendly. The temple's design incorporates locally sourced materials such as sandstone, marble, and wood, which are readily available and sustainable. The use of these materials not only provides a traditional and authentic look to the temple but also ensures that the construction process does not harm the environment.

Furthermore, the temple has been constructed using traditional building techniques such as lime mortar and stone cladding, which are eco-friendly and require minimal maintenance. These techniques ensure that the building has a longer life span, which is a key aspect of sustainable architecture.

The temple's design also incorporates natural ventilation and lighting, which reduces the need for artificial lighting and cooling. The temple's layout and orientation have been designed to maximize the use of natural light and ventilation, thereby reducing energy consumption.

Additionally, the temple has incorporated the use of renewable resources such as solar energy. The temple's management has installed solar panels to generate electricity, reducing the temple's carbon footprint and ensuring that it is self-sufficient in terms of energy consumption.

The Ram Mandir embodies the principles of environmental sustainability through its use of renewable resources and traditional building methods. The temple's management has taken measures to ensure that the construction process and the temple's operations have a minimal impact on the environment. By incorporating traditional techniques, using locally sourced materials, and incorporating renewable resources, the Ram Mandir sets an example for sustainable architecture and serves as a model for future construction projects.

Ram Mandir and Economic Development:

How the Ram Mandir can contribute to economic development and growth, including its potential to attract tourists and promote local industries.

The construction of the Ram Mandir in Ayodhya has the potential to contribute to economic development and growth in several ways, including its ability to attract tourists and promote local industries.

One of the primary economic benefits of the Ram Mandir is its potential to attract tourists from all over the world. Millions of devotees of Lord Ram visit Ayodhya every year to pay their respects at the temple, and the construction of the new temple is expected to attract even more visitors. This increase in tourism will lead to the creation of new jobs, particularly in the hospitality and tourism sectors, providing a boost to the local economy.

The construction of the Ram Mandir is also expected to create opportunities for local industries, particularly those involved in the construction and manufacturing sectors. Local businesses that provide building materials and supplies, such as sandstone and marble, are expected to benefit from increased demand, as are businesses involved in transportation and logistics.

The construction of the Ram Mandir can have a ripple effect on the local economy. The increased tourism and economic activity generated by the temple can lead to the growth of businesses, such as resturants & cultural centres, providing further opportunities for local entrepreneurs.

Furthermore, the Ram Mandir can contribute to economic development and growth through its promotion of local arts and crafts. The temple's construction has utilized local artisans and craftsmen, who have employed traditional techniques and skills to create intricate carvings and sculptures. This use of local talent and resources not only provides employment opportunities but also helps to preserve traditional art forms and crafts, contributing to the cultural heritage of the region.

The construction of the Ram Mandir in Ayodhya has the potential to contribute to economic development and growth by attracting tourists, promoting local industries, and providing employment opportunities. The temple can catalyze economic growth, particularly in the hospitality and tourism sectors, and can have a positive impact on the local economy by promoting local arts and crafts.

Ram Mandir and Cultural Heritage:

How the Ram Mandir is a vital part of India's cultural heritage, and how its preservation can promote cultural identity and pride.

The Ram Mandir is a vital part of India's cultural heritage and is an important symbol of the country's rich history and cultural identity. The temple's significance lies not only in its religious importance but also in its cultural and historical value.

The Ram Mandir is associated with the epic Ramayana, one of India's most enduring cultural and literary works. The story of Lord Ram, who is believed to have been born in Ayodhya, is an integral part of India's cultural identity, and the temple serves as a tangible reminder of this heritage. The temple's architecture and design reflect the country's cultural traditions and values, providing a visual representation of India's cultural heritage.

The preservation of the Ram Mandir is essential to promote cultural identity and pride. The temple serves as a symbol of India's past and represents the country's cultural diversity and religious pluralism. The temple's construction and preservation provide an opportunity to showcase India's rich heritage and cultural traditions to the world.

Moreover, the temple's preservation is essential to ensure the continuation of traditional art forms and crafts. The temple's construction has utilized local artisans and craftsmen, who have employed traditional techniques and skills to create intricate carvings and sculptures. The preservation of the temple ensures that these skills and traditions are not lost and are passed on to future generations.

The Ram Mandir also plays a crucial role in promoting religious tolerance and unity. The construction of the temple, which has been the subject of a long-standing dispute between different religious communities, provides an opportunity for reconciliation and promotes a sense of unity among different communities.

The Ram Mandir is a vital part of India's cultural heritage and is an essential symbol of the country's cultural identity and pride. Its preservation provides an opportunity to showcase India's rich heritage and cultural traditions to the world and promotes religious tolerance and unity. The temple's preservation ensures the continuation of traditional art forms and crafts and contributes to the cultural and historical legacy of the country.

Ram Mandir and Interfaith Relations:

How the Ram Mandir can foster interfaith dialogue, understanding, and cooperation, and how it can contribute to building a more peaceful and harmonious world.

The Ram Mandir can play a significant role in fostering interfaith dialogue, understanding, and cooperation, and can contribute to building a more peaceful and harmonious world. Here are some ways in which this can be achieved:

Promoting Religious Tolerance: The construction of the Ram Mandir can serve as a powerful symbol of religious tolerance and inclusivity. The temple's construction and preservation provide an opportunity for different religious communities to come together and engage in meaningful dialogue and cooperation. It can help create an environment where people from different faiths can respect each other's beliefs and values, and work towards building a more harmonious society.

Encouraging Interfaith Dialogue: The Ram Mandir can become a platform for interfaith dialogue, bringing together people from different faiths to discuss their beliefs and values. Interfaith dialogue can help build understanding and promote mutual respect and cooperation. The temple can be used as a venue for organizing interfaith events, such as conferences, workshops, and discussions, where people from different faiths can come together to share their perspectives and experiences.

Building Bridges of Understanding: The construction of the Ram Mandir can help bridge the gap between different religious communities. It can create an environment where people from different faiths can come together and learn from each other's beliefs and values. This can help break down stereotypes and prejudices and foster a deeper sense of understanding and empathy.

Promoting Peaceful Coexistence: The construction of the Ram Mandir can contribute to building a more peaceful and harmonious world. It can help create an environment where people from different faiths can live and work together in peace and harmony, respecting each other's beliefs and values. It can help promote a culture of peace and non-violence, which is essential for building a more just and equitable world.

Advancing Global Peace: The Ram Mandir can serve as an inspiration for people around the world to work towards building a more peaceful and harmonious world. It can become a symbol of hope and unity, promoting the idea that people from different faiths can live and work together in peace and harmony. The temple's construction and preservation can be seen as a step towards advancing global peace and understanding.

The Ram Mandir can play a vital role in fostering interfaith dialogue, understanding, and cooperation, and can contribute to building a more peaceful and harmonious world. The temple can become a symbol of religious tolerance, inclusivity, and peace, inspiring people around the world to work towards a more just and equitable society.

Ram Mandir and Good Governance:

How the Ram Mandir embodies the principles of good governance, including transparency, accountability, and citizen participation.

The construction and management of the Ram Mandir can be seen as a reflection of the principles of good governance, including transparency, accountability, and citizen participation. Here's how:

Transparency: The construction of the Ram Mandir has been a highly transparent process, with regular updates provided to the public about the progress of the project. The temple trust has been open about the sources of funding and has invited public donations to support the construction of the temple. This transparency ensures that the public is aware of the sources and uses of funds, and helps build trust in the project.

Accountability: The temple trust has taken steps to ensure that it remains accountable to the public. For example, it has appointed an independent auditor to audit its finances, ensuring that the funds are being used appropriately. The trust has also created a grievance redressal mechanism, allowing members of the public to raise any concerns they may have about the project. This accountability ensures that the trust is responsible for its actions and decisions and helps prevent any misuse of funds.

Citizen Participation: The construction of the Ram Mandir has been a collaborative effort, with citizens from all over the country contributing to the project. The temple trust has invited donations from the public, allowing people from all walks of life to contribute to the temple's construction. This citizen participation ensures that the project is a collective effort, with everyone having a stake in its success.

Ethical Standards: The construction of the Ram Mandir has been carried out by ethical standards. For example, the temple trust has ensured that the construction process is environmentally sustainable, using traditional building methods and renewable resources. The trust has also committed to fair labour practices, ensuring that workers are paid fair wages and work in safe conditions. This commitment to ethical standards ensures that the construction of the temple is carried out responsibly and sustainably.

Community Engagement: The construction of the Ram Mandir has involved the local community, with the temple trust working closely with residents to ensure that the project benefits the community. For example, the trust has committed to developing infrastructure in the surrounding areas, such as roads and water supply, to improve the quality of life for residents. This community engagement ensures that the project is carried out with the interests of the community in mind.

The construction and management of the Ram Mandir embodies the principles of good governance, including transparency, accountability, citizen participation, ethical standards, and community engagement. The project has been carried out responsibly and sustainably, ensuring that it benefits the community and is carried out with the interests of the public in mind. The temple can serve as a model for other public projects, demonstrating how transparency, accountability, and citizen participation can lead to successful outcomes.

Criticisms and Controversies:

criticisms and controversies surrounding the Ram Mandir, including debates over its historical and cultural significance, and how these critiques can inform ongoing efforts to promote ideal governance.

Despite the widespread support for the construction of the Ram Mandir, there have also been criticisms and controversies surrounding the project. Some of the main critiques are:

Historical and cultural significance: Some historians and scholars have criticized the construction of the Ram Mandir as an attempt to erase the complex history of the Ayodhya site and the diverse religious traditions that have existed there. They argue that the focus on constructing a Hindu temple ignores the fact that the site has been contested for centuries and that the construction of the temple could be seen as a triumphalist assertion of Hindu dominance over other religious traditions.

Political motivations: The construction of the Ram Mandir has been heavily politicized, with some arguing that it is a ploy by the ruling Bharatiya Janata Party (BJP) to consolidate Hindu votes ahead of elections. Critics argue that the government's involvement in the project undermines the independence of the temple trust and raises questions about the government's commitment to secularism and religious pluralism.

Economic impact: Some have raised concerns about the economic impact of the construction of the Ram Mandir. Critics argue that the vast sums of money being poured into the project could be better spent on more pressing social and economic issues, such as education and healthcare.

Environmental impact: There have also been concerns raised about the environmental impact of the construction of the Ram Mandir. Critics argue that the use of heavy machinery and the massive amount of construction materials being transported to the site could hurt the local ecology.

These critiques raise important questions about the construction and management of the Ram Mandir and highlight the need for ongoing efforts to promote ideal governance. Some possible ways to address these concerns are:

Foster dialogue and understanding: To address concerns about the historical and cultural significance of the Ram Mandir, it is important to promote dialogue and understanding among different religious communities. This can be done through interfaith initiatives, cultural exchange programs, and other forms of engagement that promote mutual respect and understanding.

Ensure transparency and accountability: To address concerns about political motivations and economic impact, it is important to ensure transparency and accountability in the management of the temple trust. This can be done through regular audits, public reporting, and the establishment of an independent oversight body to monitor the project.

Promote sustainability: To address concerns about the environmental impact of the project, it is important to promote sustainability in the construction and management of the Ram Mandir. This can be done by using eco-friendly materials and construction methods, implementing waste management and recycling programs, and promoting energy efficiency.

Ensure community participation: To address concerns about the economic impact of the project, it is important to ensure community participation in the construction and management of the Ram Mandir. This can be done by involving local communities in the decision-making process, providing opportunities for local employment and training, and investing in local infrastructure and development.

while the construction of the Ram Mandir has been widely celebrated as a symbol of national unity and cultural pride, it is important to recognize and address the criticisms and controversies surrounding the project. By promoting transparency, accountability, sustainability, and community participation, ongoing efforts can be made to ensure that the construction and management of the Ram Mandir embodies the principles of ideal governance.

Conclusion:

Summarize the key themes and ideas covered, and reflect on how the Ram Mandir can serve as a model for ideal governance, promoting social justice, environmental sustainability, economic development, and interfaith harmony.

The construction of the Ram Mandir in Ayodhya, India is a story that embodies a wide range of themes and ideas related to good governance, social justice, environmental sustainability, economic development, and interfaith harmony.

One of the key themes is transparency and accountability. The Ram Mandir project was managed by a temple trust that was responsible for overseeing the construction process and ensuring that it was carried out in a transparent and accountable manner. The trust was made up of representatives from all religious communities in Ayodhya, ensuring that the project was inclusive and representative of the diverse religious traditions in the area. The trust was also accountable to the people of Ayodhya, who were kept informed about the progress of the project and had the opportunity to provide feedback and input.

Another important theme is citizen participation. The Ram Mandir project was not simply imposed on the people of

Ayodhya. Instead, the temple trust actively sought the input and participation of residents in the planning and construction process. This not only helped to ensure that the project reflected the needs and values of the local community, but it also created a sense of ownership and investment in the project among the people of Ayodhya.

The Ram Mandir project also embodies principles of social justice. The temple trust recognized that the construction of the temple would require significant resources and investment, and they were determined to ensure that the project would benefit the entire community, especially marginalized and disadvantaged groups. The project generated thousands of jobs for residents, many of whom were trained in traditional building methods and eco-friendly construction techniques. The project also created economic opportunities for local industries, such as textiles and handicrafts. Additionally, the temple trust partnered with local organizations to provide education, healthcare, and other essential services to marginalized communities in Ayodhya.

Environmental sustainability is another important theme of the Ram Mandir project. The temple trust recognized that the construction of the temple would have an impact on the environment, and they were determined to minimize that impact as much as possible. They used eco-friendly construction techniques and traditional building methods that were more sustainable and less resource-intensive than modern construction methods. They also took steps to protect local ecosystems and wildlife habitats and to minimize waste and pollution from the construction site.

Finally, the Ram Mandir project embodies principles of interfaith harmony. The temple trust recognized that the site of the temple was contested and had been the source of religious and cultural conflict for centuries. They saw the construction of the temple as an opportunity to promote understanding, dialogue, and cooperation between different religious communities in Ayodhya. The trust organized cultural events and invited representatives from different religious communities to share their traditions and beliefs. The Ram Mandir became a symbol of cultural heritage and pride for the Hindu community, but it also served as a space for interfaith dialogue and understanding.

The Ram Mandir project is a model for ideal governance, promoting social justice, environmental sustainability, economic development, and interfaith harmony. Through transparency, accountability, citizen participation, social justice, environmental sustainability, and interfaith harmony, the project has demonstrated how a contested site can be transformed into a symbol of cultural heritage and pride, while also promoting unity, justice, and sustainability.

Synopsis

"Ram - God or Good Governance" is a thought-provoking book that delves into the dual identity of Lord Ram as a religious figure and a symbol of perfect governance. The author explores the multifaceted persona of Ram, his qualities, and how his principles of governance make him an embodiment of perfection.

The book begins by introducing the readers to the life of Ram, his teachings, and his legacy as a religious figure. The author also examines the concept of the existence of God, and how Ram embodies the ideal qualities of a divine being.

The concept of the Creator is explored in-depth, and the author argues that the principles of good governance are the very same principles that make a divine being worthy of worship. The author also explores the role of Ram in shaping Indian culture and his impact on society.

Moving on, the book highlights the qualities of governance that make Ram a symbol of perfection. The author emphasizes that governance should be based on justice, compassion, and accountability, and these are the same principles that Ram Rajya stands for.

The book argues that Ram is beyond a religious figure, and his principles of governance are universal and applicable to all societies. The author highlights how Ram Rajya can promote a sustainable and inclusive world, and how the principles of good governance can benefit humanity as a whole.

The book also elaborates on why Ram Mandir embodies the principles of ideal governance. The author examines the history of Ram Mandir, the controversy surrounding it, and how the construction of the temple represents a triumph of justice and truth over falsehood and injustice.

In conclusion, "Ram - God or Good Governance" is a fascinating book that explores the duality of Ram's identity as a religious figure and a symbol of perfect governance. The book highlights the importance of good governance, justice, and compassion in building a sustainable and inclusive world, and how Ram Rajya can serve as a model for ideal governance.

Author Bio

The author of "Ram - God or Good Governance" is a remarkable woman in her late thirties, who has travelled extensively across the globe and has a deep passion for exploring different cultures and philosophies. She believes in the power of positive thinking. "The Mind is Everything, what you think; you Become" has been a guiding principle in her life.

With an MBA from a reputed institute, the author's insatiable curiosity has led her to pursue various courses from renowned institutions, including the Dalai Lama's Tushita to Religion, Conflict & Peace Management from Harvard. Her quest for knowledge has also taken her on spiritual journeys, where she has delved deep into the teachings of various spiritual masters.

As a part of the Transforming India, Transforming World Mission, the author has been actively involved in social and political initiatives aimed at creating an equitable society. Her diverse experiences and insights have enabled her to offer a unique perspective on the intersection of religion and governance in "Ram - God or Good Governance."

Know more about Manmeet by visiting
www.manmeetsaini.com

Printed by Libri Plureos GmbH in Hamburg, Germany